Counting The Cost

The Life of Alexander Mack

Counting The Cost

The Life of Alexander Mack

1679-1735

William G. Willoughby

The Brethren Press, Elgin, Ill.

Softback Edition:

   Cover design and map by Ken Stanley

   Cover portrait of Alexander Mack, Sr. by Shirley Henley, commissioned for the Christian Hall of Fame, Canton Baptist
   Temple, Canton, Ohio. Used by permission.

   The origin of the Mack seal (cover, back) is attributed to either
   Alexander Mack or Alexander Mack, Jr. The combination
   of the cross, the heart and the fruit symbolizes the Brethren
   ideal of a devoted, fruit-bearing, sacrificial life.

Photos by Wilbur Brumbaugh

Library of Congress Catalog in Publication Data

Willoughby, William G   1917-
      Counting the cost.

      Bibliography: p.
      Includes index.
      1.   Mack, Alexander, 1679-1735.   2.   Church of the
Brethren—Biography.   3.   Church of the Brethren—
History.   I.   Title.
BX7843.M33W54   286′.5   [B]   79-462
ISBN 0-87178-159-X

DEDICATION

To Lena

My best friend and
loving wife.

The signature of Alexander Mack on a letter
written in 1711 to Count Charles August.

TABLE OF CONTENTS

PREFACE

The writing of Alexander Mack's biography has been hampered by a paucity of materials. Mack's modesty, and the reluctance of the early Brethren to glorify their leaders, inhibited them from recording much of their own history. Consequently, there are many gaps which appear in his story, and mysteries which remain unsolved. On the basis of historical knowledge, freedom has occasionally been taken, therefore, to interpret Mack's thought and action. There is substantial evidence, however, for such interpretations, and small possibility for serious violations of the truth. Hopefully, this book is faithful to Mack's life, and does not distort his personality or convictions.

It was my intention to retain the original spelling of personal names, the spelling used most frequently by the persons involved or by contemporary writers; but in order to avoid confusion among Brethren readers, I have adopted the modernized spelling used by Donald Durnbaugh in his resource books on Brethren history.

It was difficult to select an appropriate name for the early Brethren. In Germany, they called themselves "Schwarzenau Baptists" or "New Baptists." In colonial America they called themselves "Brethren" or "German Baptists." They were the indigenous Baptist movement in Germany, and for most of their history used the title "German Baptist Brethren." I have generally chosen to use the titles they themselves used in the various locations where they settled.

Where direct quotations reveal a helpful historical understanding, I have used them. The references, though kept to a minimum, may be of use to those who want to read further in the original sources.

Was Mack the "founder" of the Brethren? Although he has often been called the founder, he did not want that title. The early Brethren did not bestow honorific titles upon specific individuals. Out of respect for these attitudes, I have not used such titles in this book. Yet, in the ordinary sense of the term, Mack was, in truth, the founder of the Brethren.

I am deeply indebted to many people, but especially to Hermann Brunn of Schriesheim, Germany, for revealing Mack's genealogy and heritage from 1560 to his birth in 1679; to Heinz Renkewitz for his definitive biography of Ernest Christopher Hochmann von Hochenau; to Donald Durnbaugh for his exhaustive research in early Brethren history and his personal encouragement and support; but most of all to my wife, Lena, who traveled with me on a pilgrimage through Europe, tracing Mack's life, and posed many incisive questions which helped clarify the story and make it more readable.

I wish to pay a special tribute to my grandfather, George N. Falkenstein, who stimulated my lifelong interest in Brethren history and in Alexander Mack the man. When serving as the first paid pastor of the Germantown church, he collected and displayed memorabilia from the earliest period and wrote one of the first histories of the German Baptist Brethren. E. Miller Peterman, my Sunday-school teacher in the Harrisburg, Pennsylvania, church, was also influential in helping me see the relevance of Mack's life and thought for the present day.

Others who have been most gracious in helping me with this project are: Roswitha Brooks, Kathleen Irace, and Rhoda Kachuck, who read the first draft and made many helpful suggestions, and Linda Tapley, who typed and retyped the manuscript. Many others were extremely encouraging and helpful. The University of La Verne granted me a sabbatical leave during the spring of 1978 for finishing my research in Germany, Holland, and Pennsylvania.

To follow Mack's footsteps from his birthplace in Schriesheim to his burial place in Germantown, and then to write this book, has been my own pilgrimage of faith. Mack has sometimes repelled me, sometimes fascinated me, and often surprised me. In spite of his many weaknesses, he left a vision of caring Christian community that still tantalizingly eludes us.

William G. Willoughby
University of La Verne
1979 (The 300th anniversary
of Mack's birth)

INTRODUCTION

In Christianity, as in other religions, there are recurring periods of restless disenchantment, examination, and renewal—periods in which there emerges a faith vision which is so dynamic that it radically changes established patterns of thought for all time. New symbols and myths arise as old ones lose their power. Experimentation, conflict, hope, doubt, and a kind of divine inspiration all merge to transform and revitalize religious life.

During such periods of religious upheaval, bold new leaders challenge cherished assumptions and raise disturbing questions. Some leaders are revolutionary and charismatic, some antiestablishment, and some uniquely prophetic. The more gifted write inspired literature, highly regarded and carefully studied by later generations. A few experience visions significant enough to influence the course of human history. Others, unfortunately, are self-seeking charlatans or unscrupulous individuals who are more destructive than redemptive.

Such periods of transformation and growth are usually separated by longer interludes when religious observances and traditions are generally honored, and when dogma is seldom challenged. The vitality and spontaneous joy of spiritual renewal gives way relatively quickly to routine obligations and stabilized patterns of worship. Religious leaders then become rather traditional, primarily involved in the survival of a predictable, orderly way of life revolving around already-established institutions. At worst, they are egocentric, ambitious, and dull. At their best they work compassionately and untiringly to meet the spiritual needs of their people.

The Reformation of the sixteenth century was an era of renewal and radical change. Under the leadership of Martin Luther, John Calvin, Ulrich Zwingli, and others, a new spirit gave birth to the Lutheran and Reformed churches. At the same time Anabaptism developed under the leadership of Menno Simons, Conrad Grebel, and others; it opposed infant baptism. This movement sought to reinstitute a purified form of Christianity patterned after the New

Testament model, and gave rise to the Mennonites, the Amish, and other similar religious groups.

The Reformation was followed by more than a century of institutional religion in which the state churches, seeking to stabilize and enhance their positions of political power, used diplomacy, coercion, and even war to accomplish their purpose. Some of the pastors ministered in a loving, caring way, but many of the ecclesiastics struggled for personal status, caring little for the welfare of the people in the pews.

The end of the seventeenth century ushered in an era of renewal similar to the Reformation. Appalled by the spiritual sterility and the immoral conduct of the established church leaders, and disenchanted by a century of religious conflict, prophetic voices began to cry out for a more vital faith. In the German states, groups of spiritually sensitive people began to gather in their homes for Bible study and prayer. Thus Pietism was born. From approximately 1680 to 1740, these Pietists sought to recover the first fine rapture of the early Christian experience. Through personal piety, biblical studies, and small group worship, they strove to rise above the cold rigidity and the unethical behavior of their state churches.

In Germany, the small village of Schriesheim was a microcosmic example of the religious currents of the age. Located about five miles north of Heidelberg and twelve miles east of Mannheim, it shared both the tumultuous changes of the Reformation and a century of "institutional religion." In 1705-1706, within its own borders, it witnessed a Pietistic revival. Inspired by the religious fervor of leaders such as Gottfried Arnold, August Herman Francke, and Philip Jacob Spener, some of Schriesheim's local Christians eagerly followed the Pietistic example of one of their own young men, the twenty-six-year-old miller, Alexander Mack.

Mack was a revolutionary leader. His youthful spirit was fanned by the flame of Pietistic zeal to oppose the established church and work for radical religious change. In the course of a few years, however, his religious development led him to become a more conservative leader in his religious community.

This book is an interpretation of Mack's life, of its impact upon many other people, and of the subtle changes he made in his style of leadership. Throughout his life, Mack pursued a dream—a dream which never dimmed, though his understanding of it was continuously modified by new insight and experience.

CHAPTER I

A Century of Heritage
1560-1679

High above the German agricultural village of Schriesheim stand
the ruins of an ancient castle. For centuries it has towered above the
beautiful Rhine valley, oblivious to the seasonal planting and harvest,
the blessing of peace and the destruction of war, the arrival of immigrants and the flight of fugitives.

More than a century before Alexander Mack's birth, his great-
great-grandfather, Ebert Mack,[1] a miller by trade, settled in
Schriesheim. No doubt he was attracted by the tumbling streams
which originated in the mountains nearby to flow through the village
toward the valley below. Thirteen mills, two of which belonged at
various times to the Mack family, were scattered along these moun-
tain streams. In 1560, Ebert Mack purchased a mill not far from the
castle ruins, where he hoped to build a prosperous milling business.

Dating from 764 AD, Schriesheim was one of the oldest towns in
the German Palatinate, widely known as an agricultural center and
milling town. Nestled against the protective *Oldenwald,* a range of
rolling, thickly forested mountains to the east, it faced on the west a
flat plain four hundred square miles in area. An ancient village myth
told of a sorcerer who, when taken prisoner by a powerful king, had
drained a gigantic lake in order to secure his freedom, thus forming
this fertile plain. The real sorcerer, however, was the Rhine River,
which had gradually drained and leveled the area, making it a rich
agricultural land. Schriesheim was strategically located to provide
milling service for the grain farmers on this plain.

Ebert Mack may have been interested in finding a supportive
religious environment as well. No available records indicate why he
moved to Schriesheim, but the religious conflict of the period could

have driven him from a Catholic or a Lutheran area. In 1566, shortly before his arrival, Schriesheim changed from a Catholic to a Reformed (Calvinist) village. In harmony with Calvinistic practice, all paintings, statues, candles, and crosses were removed from the local church. Dancing and entertainment were strictly forbidden. Church attendance became obligatory and special officers were appointed by the church to enforce the law. Life in the village became a somber and serious observance. Mack, being a good Calvinist, and believing that this life is primarily a time of preparation for a future life, firmly supported the new moral and religious order.

Attractive as Schriesheim may have been to Ebert Mack, it was also a very vulnerable village. The legions of Caesar had crossed this plain, followed in turn by the crisscrossing armies of French, German, and Swedish generals. More than most others, the area surrounding Schriesheim had been pillaged, exploited, and devastated by invading armies, the castle ruins on the hill bearing mute witness to the destruction.

Because of its location at the base of the mountains, Schriesheim was also subject to occasional floods. People living by the millstreams had reason to be concerned whenever rains enveloped the mountains. On July 14, 1764, a sudden cloudburst dumped so much water in the hills that the rushing torrents seriously damaged many residences and businesses, including the mill in which Alexander Mack later lived.

Since the period from 1560 to 1600 was marked by unusual stability, peace, and prosperity, Ebert Mack escaped the effect of wars, floods, and religious intolerance. His milling business flourished and expanded, so much so that, winning the respect and the trust of his fellow citizens, he was appointed their mayor in 1594. During his term in office, ancient customs were carefully observed, religious traditions were cherished, and the Calvinist doctrines preached by Pastor Wolfgang Diehl were unquestioningly and devoutly accepted.

The seventeenth century ushered in a period of recurrent tragedies for the citizens of Schriesheim. In 1608 a league of Protestant states had been founded. One year later a league of Catholic states followed. These two groups became involved in a power struggle culminating in thirty years of religious warfare, 1618-1648. As transgressing armies systematically despoiled the countryside, Hieronymus Mack, son of Ebert and great-grandfather of Alexander, had to cope with pilfering troops, poverty, and disease. Also a miller of considerable influence, like his father, he was appointed *Zentgraf,* or local judge, in 1624. In this position he dispensed justice in local controversies, authorized marriages, and served as the town's representative to the higher authorities in Heidelberg, the provincial capital of the Palatinate.

In 1610, George Mack, Alexander's grandfather, was born.[2] He grew to adulthood during the Thirty Years War. When he was eleven years old, two Catholic armies moved toward Schriesheim, one from Bavaria under General Tilly and the other from Holland under General Cordoba. Early in November, General Tilly quartered his army in Schriesheim. A few days later he moved on, providing temporary relief from the occupation. In the middle of November, however, Cordoba appeared with an army composed of many nationalities, including Spaniards, Italians, and Germans. He also located his quarters in Schriesheim, but soon withdrew. Again General Tilly moved in, quartering his troops with the unhappy villagers for the remainder of the winter.

A rule of war gave armies the right to demand food, lodging, services, and money from local citizens. General Tilly's army demanded all of that and more. His troops were brutal and poorly disciplined, deliberately terrorizing the town's citizens. Compounding the tragedy, Tilly's army attracted many parasitical camp followers, especially women, children, and stable boys. To escape Tilly's occupation, many families fled to Heidelberg; but Heidelberg, too, fell to Tilly. Other families, including the Mack family, fled into the mountains, hiding and camping in the thick, black forests.

The village and its people suffered greatly from this period of occupation. Stories of oppression, terror, and rape were undoubtedly carried in the memories of its citizens through several generations. Especially difficult to bear was the loss of many of their own young men who were recruited for the army of the Palatinate. Few returned alive.

Toward the end of 1622, Tilly's troops moved on. The Mack family then returned to find their home plundered and despoiled but fortunately still standing. The three bells had been stolen from the village church; the grain had been taken from Mack's mill; the town was left totally barren. Joining forces, the people restored order. Politically, the village was again under Catholic control, and its citizens were obliged to be "re-Catholicized." But by various stratagems the stalwart citizens of Schriesheim resisted this oppression and remained essentially Calvinistic. In 1625, a new terror invaded the village: Schriesheim experienced a typhus epidemic so severe that it killed more people than did the invading armies.

In December of 1631, the Protestant army of the Swedish King Gustaf, after soundly defeating General Tilly, arrived in Schriesheim with his army to prepare for the recapture of Heidelberg. The burden of housing and feeding these troops again fell on the citizens of Schriesheim and the nearby village of Ladenburg. The Swedish army remained through the winter, the spring, and the summer of 1632.

In September 1632, the Bavarian army from Heidelberg successfully carried out a surprise attack upon the Swedes by advancing upon Schriesheim from the east, through the forests and the mountains. Many houses were plundered; the church was burned; and the Mack mill was destroyed. The army withdrew leaving Schriesheim in ruins and its people facing an apparently hopeless situation. They had little money and no supplies. Many had lost all they had ever owned. Discouraged, a number of families left Schriesheim to settle in less vulnerable locations. Many homes were not rebuilt for years. Since their mill had been totally destroyed, the Mack family found makeshift quarters and attempted to rebuild for the future.

As the villagers pondered their fate, the Swedish army recouped its forces, drove the Bavarian army out of Heidelberg, and restored Protestant rule to the area. But this was not the end. After a prolonged struggle, the Bavarian army again seized power, and Catholicism was reinstated. Often, in order to survive, the inhabitants of the town had to flee to the woods. Secreting food in underground hiding places, they communally cared for one another. It was during these difficult days that Alexander Mack's grandfather, George, married and began his family. In 1636, John Philip Mack, Alexander's father, was born. Conditions continued to deteriorate. By 1639 there were no cows left in the area. Only vineyards, the forests, and an indomitable will to survive made life bearable.

The bitterness generated by all this violence seared the memories of Schriesheim's citizens. George Mack must have had many stories of heartbreak and heroism to tell his grandson, Alexander. The Thirty Years War was a time of painful change. Whenever power groups in Heidelberg shifted, local officials and policies had to adapt. Religious practices in the villages and towns were obliged to alter according to the faith of the provincial government. Yet, in spite of nearly constant upheaval, the citizens of Schriesheim persisted in their rural mode of life, cultivating their fields, harvesting their grapes, felling trees in their forests, and maintaining a quiet loyalty to Calvinism. The occasional years of peace, filled with rebuilding and consolidation, were cherished.

One such tranquil period, the three years between 1641 and 1644, provided a brief time of normalcy, but the relief was short-lived. In 1644 the German and French armies again moved into the area. This was more than the remaining citizens of Schriesheim could tolerate. Most of them fled. A few families remained, hiding furtively in their ruined homes. One of these was the George Mack family. Their mill inoperable, they lived on berries, grapes, and roots which they gathered in the fields and the forests.

Finally, after thirty years of religious warfare, the Treaty of Westphalia was signed in 1648. Peace came to an exhausted Schriesheim and a prostrate Germany. George Mack with his family gratefully joined other families in services of thanksgiving for the coming of peace. Slowly, former inhabitants returned to rebuild their damaged homes and join in the task of community restoration. Together they cleaned and repaired the two common wells, worked on the hillside vineyards, and planted new crops.

In 1650, Pastor Wiederhold was assigned to the Schriesheim parish. Men from the village collected lumber from an abandoned schoolhouse and cut oak planks from the woods to build him a simple home. The church itself was in pitiable condition. When the members were able to raise the funds, a carpenter was hired to rebuild the roof. Ten years later the interior of the church was renovated and a new bell tower was completed. The new bells were rung for the first time on Christmas Day of 1661. This was the church building in which Alexander Mack was later baptized.

Unable to rebuild or retain possession of their mill, the Mack family saw it rebuilt and operated by various other families under the legal control of civil authorities. The Macks worked instead in their vineyards on the steep hill outside the village. In 1655, George Mack was installed as mayor of Schriesheim. Seven years later his son, John Philip, father of Alexander, was married to Christina Fillbrun. As soon as possible they purchased a house next to the Schwengel fountain, a house which they retained until 1690.[3]

The respite from war was unfortunately short-lived. In 1674, invading armies involved in the Dutch War of 1672-1679 swept across the Palatinate. General Turenne and his French army brutally harassed the villages and the towns around Heidelberg. Crops were trampled, houses looted, and cows slaughtered. A miller from Schriesheim was hanged and burned by these new invaders.

On July 10, 1674, five years before Alexander Mack's birth, a large portion of Schriesheim was burned, including the city hall, two mills, and half of the houses recently and painstakingly restored, as well as the entire harvest of the surrounding fields. George Mack's house on the *Markplatz* became a temporary city hall.

When the French at last withdrew, a weary people, under the leadership of Mayor George Mack, began once more to rebuild their town. A new minister, Louis Philip Agricola, arrived to become the pastor of the Reformed church.

Despite the war, John Philip Mack prospered. With the help of an inheritance from his wife's parents and encouragement from his father the mayor, he was able to re-purchase the old family mill on June 27, 1679. It was a large mill with stables for horses, a large garden, two water courses, a grinding room, and several storage areas. Today, it is known as the *Talmühle* (Valley Mill). About a month after its purchase, Alexander Mack was born, the eighth of eleven children.

The Mack family heritage brought to Alexander a long family history intertwined with the history of Schriesheim, memories of war and poverty, and strong traditions of civic leadership. His was a family steeped in the Calvinistic faith, scarred by the ravages of war, but enjoying, at least occasionally, the prosperity of a thriving business.

When Alexander was born, prospects for the Mack mill were bright. John Philip and Christina must have had high hopes for their family, and yet they could not have foreseen the significant role which their infant son, Alexander, would play in the imminent Pietistic movement.

CHAPTER II

Years of Childhood
1679-1700

In the year of Mack's birth, Charles Louis was tolerantly ruling the German Palatinate; Louis XIV, in all his courtly· magnificence, was ruling France, while Charles II sat precariously upon the throne of England, harboring dreams of leading Britain back to Rome. An uneasy peace, the politics of ambitious kings, and the pretensions of royalty were, however, of little importance to the Mack household. Weather conditions, the size of the grain harvest, and the price of grapes were of far greater interest than politics to this hard-working family as long as public order and prosperity prevailed.

On July 27, 1679, Alexander Mack was taken by his parents to the Reformed church of Schriesheim, where Pastor Louis Agricola performed baptismal rites, christening him "Alexander," a rather common given name in Germany, in honor of his godfather and uncle, Alexander Fillbrun, postmaster of nearby Neckarhausen. As Mack grew older, most of his boyhood friends were of the same church, for since the Reformation the population of Schriesheim had been primarily Reformed. In a religious census taken while Mack was a youth, six-hundred-seventy-five citizens registered as Reformed, sixty-eight as Lutheran, sixty-five as Catholic, and twenty-four as Jews. The Mack family faithfully and regularly attended the Reformed services in the village church. Here Mack was taught the doctrines of John Calvin. At the age of thirteen he attended a class of religious instruction and memorized the Heidelberg catechism in preparation for his confirmation on Easter Sunday, 1692.

As children, Alexander and his brothers worked in the family mill and vineyards. Father Mack expected his two oldest sons, John Philip and John Jacob, to become millers and continue the family

The millstream that runs through Schriesheim
and along which Alexander Mack owned a mill.

tradition. But the third son, George Conrad, a rebellious and difficult child, was often referred to as that "cursed child," and plans for him were uncertain. There is evidence that Alexander, the fourth son, was destined to attend Heidelberg Neckar College, administered by one of his uncles. However, when the oldest brother, John Philip, died in 1689 at age twenty-four, plans for Alexander's future were suddenly changed. Instead of attending the university, he, too, would become a miller.

Father Mack, hard-working and strict, knew his business well and taught it to his sons, conscientiously attempting to serve as a model for them and for his servants. He was the undisputed lord of the mill, overseeing its operations with diligence and expecting hard work in return from his workers. Mack was a well-educated and intelligent man. He served as a member of the town council and as an elder in the Reformed church. A census taken in 1698 disclosed that he employed three male servants and a maid—more servants than any other family in Schriesheim had.

The housework was delegated, of course, to his wife. If she was like other German women, she kept her house in immaculate order, assigning responsibilities to her maid, her daughter, and her daughters-in-law, and supplying her large family with simple but ample country food. Although she was mistress of her household, she shared no equality with her husband; her authority derived from him. Loyal to him and to her Calvinistic heritage, she was careful in the use of money, refusing to indulge herself in unnecessary luxury or fashionable clothes. Hard work and thrift were her virtues—and her calling.

In 1681, when Alexander Mack was two years old, Francis Daniel Pastorius left Frankfurt to seek for opportunity in America. He settled in Pennsylvania, where he founded Germantown, near Philadelphia. That was also the year in which the French conquered and occupied the city of Strassburg on the Rhine. Becoming more and more aggressive, they moved inexorably toward the fertile Palatinate.

In 1684, the ominous year in which the French invaded Luxembourg and took possession of Trier, Peter Ewald was chosen to be the new young schoolmaster of Schriesheim. He was recognized as a very capable and superior teacher. School began in a private house, but in 1685, when this house was needed for the village wine steward, the school was moved into the Reformed church. A balcony was constructed over the chancel to serve as a classroom until better quarters could be obtained. Since this was the only church and the only school in the village, Reformed, Lutheran, and Catholic children all attended it.

From 1685 to 1693 the Schriesheimer children studied reading, writing, and arithmetic in these cramped quarters. Here Alexander Mack learned to know and respect Peter Ewald, who continued teaching in this village into his seventies, witnessing many civil and religious upheavals, including Mack's own departure from Schriesheim.

In 1685 the tolerant Prince Charles Louis died, and the Simmern line of the Palatine royal family came to an end. This circumstance precipitated a critical problem of succession. Philip William, a Catholic prince, claimed the throne and began to rule. But Louis XIV of France insisted that his sister-in-law, Liselotte, sister of the deceased Charles Louis, should be placed on the throne instead. Thus the tranquil years of peace and prosperity were threatened and Europe was soon plunged into war. By the autumn of 1686 the French armies were on the move and within a short time possessed the whole Palatinate.

One bright event in the life of Schriesheim's citizens occurred in 1687, when Mack was eight years old. The *Rathaus,* or city hall, was completed, equipped with a set of newly cast bells, and formally dedicated. In a closeknit community such as Schriesheim, and to a family so involved in its civic organization as the Macks were, this was a momentous event. Alexander's grandfather, who had served the longest tenure any mayor had ever served in Schriesheim, thirty years, lived to see this dream realized. In the following year, at age seventy-seven, he died. His funeral was a ceremonious public occasion, undoubtedly making a deep impression on the young Alexander.

Early in 1689, the war of the Grand Alliance of German and Dutch states against France reached its climax. The French government, recognizing that it had extended its boundaries too far, gave the order to withdraw, commanding its officers of the occupation to burn the Palatinate as they retreated. Hundreds of German villages and towns were systematically destroyed. Schriesheim, which had been spared the presence of French troops, was not burned, but the people were required to pay heavy tribute in money and goods to French army headquarters in Heidelberg.

Toward the end of January 1689, German forces from Bavaria moved toward Heidelberg. Volunteers from Schriesheim organized to support this thrust against the French. Engaging in a furious skirmish at Handschuhsheim, a village several miles from Schriesheim, these German volunteers were soundly defeated. Handschuhsheim was burned and pillaged by the vindictive French.

When news of this battle reached Schriesheim, its inhabitants were terrified. War was not new to them. They knew its terror and what now might happen. Most of the villagers fled through the snow and the cold to hide away in the hills for a number of weeks. A few courageous folk remained in the town, hiding what they could from the plundering armies. To safeguard their treasured *Rathaus* bells they lowered them into the village well.

On February 2, 1689, after an unsuccessful assault on Weinheim, the French General von Melac arrived in Schriesheim with his frustrated army. Tradition claims that when he found the village deserted he tried in vain to call the people back from the woods. The truth is that four of its leading citizens bribed General von Melac to spare their town. Though he had intended not to leave so much as a swine's stall standing within ten miles of Heidelberg, General von Melac did refrain from burning Schriesheim. However, before returning to Heidelberg, his troops plundered many of the vacant houses. Finally, when the Mack family returned to Schriesheim, they gratefully discovered that their mill was still standing.

With the withdrawal of the French troops, German troops began to plague the village. Repeatedly the town council paid the German troops to stay away from Schriesheim. More money was spent to placate their own German troops and protect their town than they had spent to save their village from the French. It was a difficult time. Interference of the troops cut the harvest to half its usual size. Because of fear that the French might return, *Frondienst,* or forced conscription, was imposed upon all eligible males.

In 1690, Mack's father, John Phillip, was appointed *Bürgermeister* of Schriesheim for the year, thus perpetuating a long tradition of community service in the Mack lineage. The whole family, if they were a typical Schriesheim family, were certainly highly pleased with the civic honor given Father Mack—with the possible exception of the "cursed son," George.

Another joyful event in the Mack household was the marriage of Alexander's only living sister, Anna Margaret, to John Caspar Bayer.

Since the Macks were perhaps the wealthiest family in Schriesheim, they were able to give their daughter a very handsome dowry in spite of the years of war.

About the time of the wedding, the Bavarian army moved its encampment to a location just a few miles from Schriesheim. According to one contemporary account these soldiers fell on undestroyed Schriesheim like a swarm of bees, plundering it of whatever they could find. These troops became a continuing disturbance and expense to the citizens of the village, but, in spite of this, life continued rather quietly and predictably.

In May of 1693, however, a French general with a strong army crossed the Rhine at Philippsburg and marched toward Heidelberg. Once more the people of Schriesheim hid the *Rathaus* bells in the village well, gathered together all they could carry, and fled to the hills or to distant villages. Heidelberg was completely destroyed by fire, and the ancient castle was blown up with explosives. Alexander Mack, now thirteen years of age, watched from the hills where he and his family were hiding as once again the southern sky was illuminated by the flames of war. The French occupied Heidelberg until September. Hoping to safeguard their town as they had in the past, citizens of Schriesheim sent gifts and money to the French troops. Nevertheless, once again these foreign troops were stationed in the village and were supported by local funds. When the French withdrew from the area in September, there was no relief, for a large corps of German soldiers moved in to take their place. The town was near bankruptcy from the heavy military demands. With no harvest to replenish supplies, the winter brought many families close to starvation.

In 1694, there was a repetition of the same senseless skirmishes. For the third time the *Rathaus* bells were hidden in the well. For the third time the youthful Alexander fled with his family into the hills. During this occupation the mayor of Schriesheim was shot and killed by the French. In 1696, Alexander Mack's father was again chosen to be the *Bürgermeister*. This was a dangerous, difficult, and delicate position to hold, for the people of Schriesheim now faced the unhappy plight of paying tribute to both the German and the French armies. These were chaotic years, years of poverty, years of terror, years of haphazard attempts at education and normalcy. These were the formative years of Alexander Mack's childhood.

In 1697, peace was declared, and the War of the Grand Alliance was finally over. Mack was eighteen years old, mature beyond his years because of these experiences. Half of his life had been spent in the midst of war. He had known hunger and terror. He had cowered in the woods to survive. He had returned home never knowing what he might find. Undoubtedly these years of certainty and horror contributed to Mack's unequivocal opposition as an adult to violence and war.

As a maturing young man, Mack had to think about his own future. He was made keenly aware of this when George Mack, the rebellious third son, announced his intentions of marrying Anna Margaret Schwartz from Ladenburg and leaving Schriesheim. After the wedding the Mack family bade George and Anna Margaret goodbye as they left to set up housekeeping in Ladenburg, where George could pursue his trade as a baker. The Mack family was not sorry to see George leave, for they looked upon him as a thorn in the flesh.

Both George and Alexander were rebellious against tradition, George in secular ways, Alexander in religious ways. It is quite evident that the stresses of operating the mill, the almost constant occupation by invading armies, and the pervasive insecurity of the times exacted a heavy toll from the Mack family.

With the oldest son dead, and George living away from Schriesheim, only John Jacob and Alexander were left to care for the family business. Since both sons were hard workers, their father rightfully expected them to operate the mill. But he had other expectations too! He expected Alexander to marry a good wife and have some sons.

Mack, however, was not wholeheartedly committed to being a miller. He had vague feelings of restlessness, did not have good rapport with his father, or his older brother, and was searching for something more than operating a mill. He had a very strong feeling about right and wrong. He felt cheated by the moral laxity of church leaders and by the blatant sinfulness of prominent church members. Nevertheless, with one expectation of his father he was in full agreement. He intended to get married someday.

The *Rathaus* or city hall in Schriesheim.

CHAPTER III

Years of Learning
1700-1705

During Mack's formative years a burst of religious enthusiasm called Pietism swept over northern Europe. Weary of institutional lethargy and dreary sermons analyzing fine points of church doctrine which seemed to have nothing to do with the daily life of the people, many persons in the pews yearned for a more vital religious experience. Clergymen, who seemed more preoccupied with wealth and prestige than with human needs, disenchanted many of the laity. Churches declined in influence and spiritual power. In addition, drunkenness and dissipation among church leaders in high places radically weakened the church's effectiveness.

Hungry for a genuinely satisfying spiritual life, people began to turn to popular devotional works, gathering in small groups to pursue by themselves the study of the Bible in relation to their lives. Their zest became contagious, and in an atmosphere of joyful excitement, open discussion, and religious enthusiasm, Pietism spread widely.

In 1702 or 1703, Mack became strongly attracted to the ideas and the activities of these Pietists. As early as 1700 there had been a number of Pietistic groups in the Mannheim-Heidelberg area, but they had probably not been of great significance to Mack at that time, for he was seriously involved in pursuing another interest.

On January 18, 1701, Alexander Mack, twenty-one, and Anna Margaret Kling, twenty, were married in the village church by Pastor Agricola. Their wedding may have been the social event of the year, for it united two of the most prestigious families of Schriesheim. Anna Margaret's grandfather had been a mayor of Heidelberg. Her father, John Valentine Kling, was a member of the Schriesheim town council and an elder in the church. A strict and devoted Calvinist, Kling strongly supported religious tradition and had even invited Pastor Agricola's wife to be the worthy godmother for one of his children. Following the wedding, Anna Margaret moved to the Mack mill with Alexander to become a part of his extended family.

One year later, Mack's brother, John Jacob, married Anna Catharina Engelhorn of Hockenheim and brought her home also to the mill. Thus three family units were living and working there.

Ten months after their wedding, Alexander and Anna Margaret rejoiced in the birth of their first child. Baptized in the village church on November 13, 1701, he was given the name of John Valentine, in honor of his maternal grandfather.

But their joy was soon followed by sorrow, for in the early autumn of 1702 a mourning Mack family followed on foot through the narrow winding streets behind the coffin of Alexander's mother, as it was taken to the village burial grounds. For thirty-eight years she had been married to John Phillip Mack, bearing him eleven children, of whom only four survived to become adults. Her greatest joy, perhaps, was that she lived long enough to see her four children married and to receive into her arms her first grandchild.

John Philip was bereft. Saddened by his wife's death and by his failure to develop a cohesive family unit under one roof, he decided to divide his property among his three sons. In this contract he did not include his daughter, for she had received her portion as a dowry at the time of her marriage. To Jacob, the oldest, Mack gave one-half of the mill and to Alexander the other. To George he gave a house. Explaining this decision to make a living will, he wrote:

> Because I am no longer able to continue the management of the household and employees at these difficult times, I have therefore decided to allocate all of my possession to my heirs on certain conditions: that my basic needs are cared for for the rest of my life, and that the right is reserved to me to increase, to lessen, or to cancel these provisions whenever I decide, especially if one or the other of my children does not behave toward me as is due and as children owe their parents.[1]

In his will, John Philip stressed the desire that all of his children live together in peace. Perhaps, even as he was writing, he was aware of some hidden hostility among the brothers. Perhaps he realized that the mill was too small to support two enlarging families and an ailing grandfather. Although he could write eloquently, and speak so per-suasively in the sessions of the city council that other councilmen were envious, he felt a strong sense of failure over his inability as a father to keep two of his sons in line. With some degree of anxiety he faced his remaining years.

Mack's mill might have supported two families had there been a stable peace, but in 1701 Europe engaged in another spree of madness, the War of the Spanish Succession. Once again Schriesheim suffered the consequences. From 1702 until 1716, its citizens were constantly hounded by the government for taxes to support this war, for housing for soldiers, and for supplies. Overnight, Schriesheim became once again a base for passing armies, quartering soldiers in its inns and private homes. Command headquarters were established in the *Rathaus* and bitter memories of the past were rekindled in the reality of the present.

An increasingly difficult burden for this agricultural community was the compulsory labor demanded of its citizens and their conscrip-tion for military duty. In 1702, Schriesheim had to provide and finance a contingent of six to eight men who were sent as troops to Kaiser-slautern. In 1703 it was required to send additional troops to Wessen-berg. In 1704 more men were sent to Mannheim. Others were con-scripted for labor in trenches and fortifications. Conscription was very unpopular. The job of nightwatchman in Schriesheim, which provided military exemption, was so appealing that a man would work for half his regular wages in order to secure the coveted position.

The years between 1701 and 1706 were exceptionally difficult years for the two millers. In 1704, for example, an English army marched through the village. Although allies of the Germans, they in-flicted considerable damage and assaulted a number of the village citizens. The Macks had to quarter soldiers in the mill, pay heavy tax-es to the army, and provide flour for the troops. Discouragement was a constant companion, but never in command.

In April 1703 a second son was born to Alexander and Margaret Mack. This child was baptized and christened John *(Johannes)* in the Reformed church by the aging Pastor Agricola. This is the last event to indicate any official relationship between Alexander Mack and the Reformed church of Schriesheim. It appears that Alexander Mack, as late as 1703, still maintained, outwardly at least, an acceptable relationship with his family, though a less satisfactory one with the church.

Mack was a troubled young man. In the first twenty years of his life, he had known only four years of civil peace. The death of his oldest brother at the age of ten had prevented Alexander from realizing his dream of attending Heidelberg University. Several other brothers and sisters had died. Mack must have had serious questions about his own religious condition and about the nature of God and humanity, questions which the inflexible doctrinal preaching of Agricola could not satisfy.

Perhaps the aging pastor was no longer able to provide inspiring leadership. Perhaps the religious wars of his childhood forced Mack to question traditional religion. Or perhaps the meaningless services of his village church aroused his dissatisfaction. Whatever the situation was, Mack was bent on a serious religious quest.

The local congregation was having its own internal troubles. In 1698 a Catholic priest had taken over the village church, to be followed by a Lutheran pastor one year later. Although each of the legally accepted faiths—Catholic, Reformed, and Lutheran—was permitted to use the church, with some part of the building reserved for each group, considerable dissension and bitterness developed among the three.

Pastor Agricola's zealous authoritarianism was able to keep his own congregation together. They met for worship every Sunday morning and every Wednesday evening. On Sunday afternoons the children of the church attended meetings with the pastor for doctrinal instruction. Four times a year communion was served, to which the members of the congregation responded according to rank and age. Members of the city council and the elders' body were served first. Both the Mack and the Kling men were permitted to partake early of the holy experience, but, according to the late Dr. Hermann Brunn, the Schriesheim historian, "woe to the inn keeper's wife if she went to the table of the Lord before the wife of the schoolmaster."[2]

Seating in the church services was also arranged by social class. Families rented or bought their pews and passed them down from generation to generation. The church warden was required to enforce the seating procedure, making sure that each family sat in its appropriate place each Sunday.

In spite of his flaws, Pastor Agricola made one very significant contribution to church history when he compiled a list of his predecessors dating back to the Reformation. In the eyes of some members, this accomplishment did not compensate for his lack of authentic religious fervor. From 1700 to 1705, Pastor Agricola faced the additional problem of a growing Pietistic movement within his flock—a movement he had no success in quelling.

Perhaps all of the literate members of the congregation were to some extent familiar with Pietistic pamphlets and books. One of the most widely read authors was John Arndt, a notable forerunner of Pietism. For Arndt, the essence of Christianity lay in the very real presence of the Kingdom of God experienced by Christians who modeled their lives after the life of Christ. Arndt believed that the institutional church was comparatively unimportant.

Philip Jacob Spener is usually considered the "father" of German Pietism. For a number of years he served churches at Strassburg and Frankfurt, both located in the Rhine valley not far from Schriesheim. His most important devotional work was *Pia Desideria* (Pious Desires). In this book, published in 1675, Spener encouraged Christian laymen to form their own religious groups for Bible study and prayer. He contended that knowledge of faith is not adequate; faith must be expressed through action and life in every choice and decision. Concerned about the education of the clergy, he recommended the strengthening of their personal piety and biblical scholarship. Sermons, he felt, should be vehicles for edification rather than for doctrinal instruction, and should encourage religious feelings rather than impart intellectual knowledge.

Some clergymen supported this new movement within their congregations, but most—including Pastor Agricola of Schriesheim—vigorously opposed it. The gathering together of sincerely questing laypeople beyond the authority of the church was too threatening. Spener, himself a clergyman, had no intention of starting new religious institutions. He was dedicated to the revitalization of already-established churches. Nevertheless, some lay persons found so much satisfaction and inspiration in their small-group pursuits that they refused to attend traditional services which no longer spoke to their needs. Such Pietists were called "Separatists."

From 1703 to 1705, Mack became increasingly critical of established religious institutions, indicting them for coldness, immorality, and lack of fervor. Mack was most critical of the pastor's appointment of his own son as his associate minister. Agricola arranged that, in the event of his own death, his son would become his successor.

Mack's dissatisfaction with the church of his heritage did not lead him into cynical secularism. His quest was motivated by a sincere desire for a warm and rich religious life, constantly fed by new inspiration and meaningful devotions. Perplexed and bewildered by the inequities and violence he had seen, he found all formal church doctrine inadequate to support him under the pressure of existing events. Through doubt and disillusionment he searched for a better way, a way which would supply his spiritual needs and satisfy his deepest yearnings.

One religious movement which held strong appeal for Mack was that of the Anabaptists. Some Mennonite congregations had been living in the Palatinate for many years. The earliest record of these Anabaptists is preserved in a letter written by a Palatinate minister in 1582 to the celebrated Erasmus imploring him to write a small booklet defending the Christian faith against the Anabaptists. A few years later, after ruthless persecution, many Anabaptists were executed. By the time of Alexander Mack, Mennonites were tolerated if they did not attempt to evangelize or disturb the status quo. For a number of years persons attending Anabaptist meetings were required to pay a special tax, but this form of oppression had ceased before Mack's interest in their movement developed.

Preceding as well as during Mack's lifetime, many Swiss Anabaptists fled from severe persecution to Germany. Escaping the extremely cruel and legalistic church structure of Calvinistic Switzerland, they made the Palatinate their favorite destination. German authorities, however, were not eager to welcome foreign Anabaptists into their communities. Most of these Anabaptists eventually migrated to Holland or to America.

There are very few records to trace Mack's own religious pilgrimage in detail. However, with his inquiring mind, it is inconceivable that he could have lived in the Palatinate without acquiring a thorough knowledge of the numerous Mennonite congregations. Certainly, through the denunciations leveled against them by the pastors of the Reformed Church, Mack could have acquired at least a rudimentary knowledge of their beliefs and practices. It is also quite possible that some of his customers at the mill were Mennonites.

Mack, for whatever reasons, chose not to become a Mennonite, preferring instead to identify himself with the Pietistic movement. Alexander Mack, Jr., in describing the origins of the Brethren, described early Pietistic gatherings as the impetus for those who later became the Brethren:

> Here and there private meetings (in which newly-awakened souls sought
> their edification) were established alongside of the usual church
> organizations. However, because of the spiritual envy of the clergy, the
> hearts of the authorities were embittered and persecution began to take
> place . . . .[3]

The Pietistic movement in the Palatinate gained public attention
as early as 1702 when Matthew Baumann of Lambsheim openly
voiced criticism of the established church. There are records from
1703 of an itinerant Pietist preaching to a gathering of one hundred
people in Heidelberg. In April, four Pietists of Lambsheim were imprisoned for refusing to take an oath[4] demanded of citizens. Their
possessions were confiscated and when they were released they were
driven out of the area. Two of these men, John Traut and Jacob
Bossert, eventually became part of the Baptist (Brethren) movement
in the Marienborn area, not far from Frankfurt.

Alexander Mack's conversion experience was the first major
event of his new religious life. Whatever the source of his discontent,
whatever his relationship with Pastor Agricola, whatever his disenchantment with Calvinist doctrine, like other Pietists Mack found
meaning for his life as a Christian in direct relationship to Christ.

The precipitating influence in Mack's decision was probably a
Pietistic group with which he was associated. At gatherings in
Heidelberg, Mannheim, and other neighboring villages, Mack's participation in intense Bible study and prayer convinced him that God
was calling him directly to a new life through Christ. Alexander
Mack, Jr.'s observation of the event was that God had awakened his
father "from the death and sleep of sin."[4] Anna Margaret, Mack's
wife, and others in Schriesheim were also "awakened."

Although the Bible was the Pietists' major source of divine inspiration, Alexander Mack's subsequent writings indicate that he was
familiar with both Pietistic and Mennonite literature. In his own
writings he quotes from Gottfried Arnold's book, *True Portrait of a
Christian,* a work so scholarly that Arnold was invited to become
professor of church history at the University of Giessen. Another of
Arnold's books, one to which Mack felt deeply drawn, was *Impartial
History of the Church and Heretics,* published in 1699. In this treatise
Arnold demonstrated how the established church had betrayed the
spirit of Christ, and he suggested that those who were called heretics

were the true followers of Christ's life and message. Mack was also acquainted with Jeremias Felbinger's *Christian Handbook* and the widely circulated *Martyrs' Mirror* of the Mennonites.

Perhaps the most important of all human influences on the life of Alexander Mack was Ernest Christopher Hochmann of Hochenau. Among his contemporaries, Hochmann was called many names: "free spirit," "enthusiast," "sectarian," Separatist, Quaker, and "fanatic."[5] He was one of those rare charismatic personalities who are capable of changing lives and creating new visions. Traveling throughout Germany, Hochmann, like John the Baptist, called people to repentance, preaching the boundless, unconditional love of God for humankind.

At age twenty-three, Hochmann left his home in Hamburg to study law at the University of Halle. Here, he became acquainted with some of the leading Pietists of that time, notably Professor August Hermann Francke. At Halle, Professor Francke had established an orphanage, a hospital, a seminary, a missionary society, and a Bible society, as well as several schools. During his stay at Halle, Hochmann felt the influence of this remarkable man and experienced within himself a transforming religious experience. Of this experience he wrote, "God out of pure grace opened my eyes, and brought me from darkness to his marvelous light."[6]

After a visit with Gottfried Arnold in Switzerland in 1699, Hochmann began to exert pressure upon established religious communities, calling them also to repentance. This onslaught against tradition and oppressive religious practice soon forced him to find a safe retreat in Berleburg, a few miles from Schwarzenau. There, in the spring of 1700, he established a pentecostal congregation after the "order of Melchizedek." He considered himself a minister of Christ, though he held no ordination by ecclesiastical authority. He ordained some of his followers as ministers, too.

In April 1700, Hochmann publicly repudiated the long-established practice of infant baptism, giving "spirit baptism" instead to some of the older children under his tutelage. This heresy so antagonized the Berleburg authorities that he was again forced to flee. In 1702, he was arrested and imprisoned in the castle dungeon at Detmold, where his persecutors refused to release him until he presented them with a written confession of faith. This *Confession*, written by Hochmann in the Detmold prison, was immediately published and widely circulated. According to Brethren historian M. G. Brumbaugh, this confession, "next to the Bible was the most important influence in the genesis of the church."[7] It was later published several times by the Brethren.

Following his release from prison, Hochmann journeyed to many communities throughout the German states. He conceived of himself as a prophet of God, sent to warn persons in high places of their fate and to lead them to a personal conversion before it was too late. Treated with suspicion wherever he went, and wary of continual persecution, he sought and found in the state of Wittgenstein, in the small rural village of Schwarzenau, the precious freedom of conscience he desired. Here, in 1703, he established his *Laboratorium,* a commune of likeminded persons who wished to yield body, mind, and spirit to God and to share their earthly possessions as a group. No authority was recognized in this commune except the authority of Christ. Each member, male and female, was considered equal in importance. For whatever unrecorded reason, perhaps because of its strong individualism, this commune did not last longer than a year.

Once again Hochmann found himself engaged in a traveling, preaching mission, this time through the lower Rhine valley, accompanied by the well-known Pietist, Christian Erb. With great passion, Hochmann called people to lift the burden of institutionalized religion from their backs in order that they might walk freely as children of God.

It is quite possible that Mack met Hochmann at Mannheim, where the millers of Schriesheim delivered their flour. Perhaps he attended one of Hochmann's preaching missions in the lower Rhine valley. Whatever the occasion, Mack came under the influence of Hochmann's power and was strongly attracted by his faith in the boundless love of God and his compassion for those who longed for freedom from oppression.

By the year 1704, Alexander and Margaret had become increasingly and painfully uncomfortable with the Reformed Church, feeling less and less obliged to continue their outward forms of loyalty. Though this was a punishable offense, they occasionally attended some church other than their own on Sunday mornings. Drawn by the enthusiasm of the Pietists, they courageously, though dangerously, participated in some of their private gatherings.

Finally, influenced by both Arnold and Hochmann, Alexander Mack made his second major religious decision: he could no longer conscientiously remain associated with the established church. In character with this decision he withdrew functionally from membership and identified himself openly as a Pietistic Separatist. This was not an easy decision to make. In the institutional church, where many of his family and friends remained, his position was considered beyond salvation or hope. By doing this, he automatically cut himself off from being appointed to a civil position. Yet Mack's yearning for meaningful truth, the restlessness of his sensitive conscience, and his own subjective experiences of God through Christ proved stronger than family ties or economic success. He literally forsook family, friends, and a vocational future in order to be true to the inner voice of God's Spirit as he understood its revelation to him—a leap of faith into a mysterious unknown.

CHAPTER IV

A Time of Separation
1705-1706

Pietism grew rapidly. Pietists who did not withdraw from the established churches were often tolerated by pastors who simply ignored their group gatherings in homes. Those Pietists who continued to attend Sunday services, partake in communion, and work from within to renew the church, were permitted to remain as members in good standing.

But the Separatists, who no longer supported the church nor attended communion, were viewed as a serious threat to the established church and often faced public persecution. In 1705, following his introduction to Hochmann, Mack joined ranks with the Separatists. Twenty-six years old, with a wife and two children to provide for, Mack found himself irresistibly drawn into conflict with his brother and his father. Stimulated by the religious insight which brought him much joy, and committed to a dream which allowed him no compromise with a corrupt and apostate institution, Mack began to cut ties with his family and his past. Respect for his father, whose health was rapidly failing, kept Mack from expressing his religious convictions overtly. His father believed Pietistic activities were acts of disobedience against the church. Even the overt waywardness of his son, George, the baker, was more acceptable to Father Mack than the radical religious "fanaticism" of Alexander's weekly meeting with his wife and friends for Bible study. John Philip's dream for his sons crumbled in lamentable disappointment.

In spite of his father's displeasure, Mack was so drawn to his newfound faith that he began to separate himself from the burdensome responsibilities of mill ownership. On March 5, 1706, he sold his half of the family mill to his brother Jacob,[1] retaining only the right to use one large room and the kitchen for ten years. With this sale, Mack's father recognized the firm determination of Alexander to continue in his Pietistic direction. Disappointed, and perhaps bitter, he died the following June at age seventy.

Despite their differences of opinion concerning religion, Alexander Mack attended the funeral service in the village church and mourned with the rest of his family the loss of his father. With intense sadness, mixed perhaps with feelings of guilt for the pain he had brought to his family, Mack walked in the funeral cortege with his wife, his brothers, and his sister to pay his last respects.

Mack did not wait long, thereafter, to give himself unreservedly to his religious activities. Soon after his father's funeral, he set out to participate in a mission in the Marienborn area with Hochmann and Erb. In August of 1706, at Mack's urgent invitation, Hochmann, Erb, and other Pietists arrived in Schriesheim to be greeted with enthusiasm by the Pietists there, possibly including Anna Margaret's father, John Valentine Kling. Although Kling never openly repudiated the established church, he later became an ardent Pietist.

There must have been an intense emotional reaction to the arrival of a leader like Hochmann in that small village. To those persons who had found renewed faith and forgiveness in this new movement, Hochmann's visit must have evoked great joy and anticipation, mixed perhaps with concern for the consequences. But Pastor Agricola and his son, along with church elders and members of the city council, met this challenge with suspicion, anger, and fear. Hochmann's charisma was a very real threat to the leadership of all who were charged with defending and preserving the sanctity and the authority of the church.

Not willing to confine their activities to small gatherings in homes, Hochmann and Erb engaged in persuasive street preaching. They distributed literature to workers returning from the fields in the evening, and confronted people with their message of God's redeeming love wherever opportunity arose.

The success of their mission and the contagion of their joy caused the Reformed church council in Heidelberg (on August seventh) to call upon the government to stop "this evil before it spreads further."[2] They complained that "so-called Pietists have been getting the upper hand in the city . . . and especially in Schriesheim."

On August 22, Hochmann and Erb led a gathering of Pietists in Mack's mill. Responding to a request from the Reformed church council, Heidelberg's chief law enforcement officer, of the name of Schumm, attended their meeting. He interrogated the members harshly to determine if they had indeed engaged in illegal activities. The county clerk, who accompanied this officer, was so violently incensed by the Pietist heresy that he threatened to call in a regiment of soldiers to put them all under arrest. Mack had to make a very quick decision whether to flee or to remain. Choosing to flee, he and his family hastily gathered together their most indispensable possessions and went out into the night to escape prosecution.

Reporting back to the Palatine authorities at Heidelberg, Schumm estimated that there were at least fifty active Pietists in Schriesheim who would, he said, "certainly have gained a majority, and captured many hundred souls in a short time if we had not gone in person to the scene . . . to disrupt and drive away this heretical pack."[3]

Once again Alexander Mack fled from Schriesheim, repeating the pattern of his early childhood when he fled from the scourge of war. Taking only what they could carry, he and his wife, with their two small sons, trudged through the hilly vineyards, over the winding back roads, toward Heidelberg, hoping to find refuge there with families of similar faith.

To their dismay, they found that the situation in Heidelberg was no better than in Schriesheim. Recently vandals had thrown rocks through the window of a home where a Pietistic gathering was in session.

Where could the Mack family go? They may have pushed on to Zuzenhausen, where a gracious Mennonite, Hans Bechtolt, had welcomed eleven other refugees from Schriesheim—including Erb and Hochmann. But under the threat of Bechtolt's arrest, the group returned to Heidelberg. Not able to remain safely in any one place for long, Hochmann, Erb, and others fled to Mannheim. Mack and his family chose to remain in the vicinity of Heidelberg to await further developments.

On September 6, civil authorities broke into a Pietistic meeting at Mannheim and arrested all those who were present. Hochmann, Erb, and Martin Lucas (who would figure in Brethren history at a later date) were among those arrested and thrown into prison. On the following day these prisoners were brought before the city council for questioning.

The views expressed by Hochmann, Erb, and Lucas during this

interrogation were very similar to the views held by Alexander Mack at this particular time. When asked to identify the church to which he belonged, Erb replied that he was not "making a new religion, but only seeking to unite himself with God."[4] When the council asked Erb why he did not worship in one of the three legally recognized churches, Erb responded that he did not find that any of these churches generated the love of God in the lives of their members.

When it was Hochmann's turn to speak in his own defense he insisted that he was not preaching new doctrines, but rather the ancient teaching of Jesus Christ. He called the churches "outward churches" in contrast to Christ's church, the true temple of worship. When he was questioned about his presence in Schriesheim, Hochmann contended that those who attacked him for being there were really attacking God, for Hochmann was a son of God who had come to Schriesheim to honor God and Christ and to call the people to repentance.

Erb and Hochmann were questioned vigorously about their evangelistic activity, including their authority for misleading the poor and inciting them to disobey their government. Hochmann's reply expressed one of the basic tenets of German Separatists: "When the government orders something that is against the will of God, people need not respect and obey it."[5]

As the interrogation continued, the authorities discovered that Hochmann and Erb carried passports identifying them as members of God's Kingdom, passports requesting local governments to grant them friendship and tolerance. This discovery infuriated the civil authorities, whose legal right to issue passports had been scorned. Martin Lucas, the buttonmaker from Heidelberg, had a simple answer when these angry civil servants cast their accusations against him. He simply wanted to be a Christian!

On the afternoon of their trial, when a friend from Heidelberg arrived requesting permission to visit them, he was promptly jailed also. On the following day, September 8, Alexander Mack came to the Mannheim prison with the same request. Because the prisons were full, he was rudely expelled from the city.

Reports of these Pietistic arrests and interrogations were sent to the ruler of the Palatinate. Determined to stamp out the Pietistic movement in his territory at any cost, he issued a decree on September 14 that all Pietists found in such illegal gatherings be seized and put to hard labor without hearing or trial. The Mannheim civil authorities were glad to support this decree: Hochmann and others were sent out of the city to work on the fortifications along the Neckar River "in the hope that others of their ilk would be intimidated."[6]

The opposite outcome occurred. People flocked from great distances to hear Hochmann preach, spending the entire day by the Neckar River to be in his presence. Guards assigned to the group were powerless; they could neither prevent Hochmann's preaching nor the people's gathering to listen. Crowds rose repeatedly to the defense of the prisoners, declaring their punishment unjust. A military contingent had to be called to disperse the crowd, a contingent which brutally assaulted the prisoners.

That night the bruised and battered prisoners were visited by the sympathetic pastor and elders of the Reformed church. They attempted to console the Pietists and promised to write letters on their behalf to the Palatinate government in Heidelberg. Their suffering drew the Reformed church members of Mannheim closer together and an intense religious revival took place among them, with wide support being given to Hochmann and his followers. The Mannheim authorities, fearing that the situation was getting out of control, sent a plea on September 21 to the Palatine authorities to enforce still harsher measures against these heretical Pietists. By this time an underground movement developed, through which religious refugees could find shelter in the homes of Mennonites and other sympathetic families. Mack and his family probably survived this way, for a while going underground.

In the meantime, Hochmann and Erb prepared and sent a persuasive petition to the Heidelberg government requesting their freedom. On September 28 the government granted them freedom on the condition that they would never return to Mannheim or to the Palatinate. Reluctantly, the authorities in Mannheim released them.

Immediately, Hochmann and Erb left for Marienborn, one of the few areas where Separatists were tolerated. By December 1, 1706 Hochmann left Marienborn to return to Schwarzenau in Wittgenstein.

Because of the severity of the Palatinate persecution, which continued unabated for several years, many Pietists migrated to Wittgenstein and the Marienborn area. Mack and his family became part of that migration. By this time Mack had developed a reputation as a Pietistic leader in his own right, not just as a follower of Hochmann.

In late 1706 the Mack family relocated in Schwarzenau, searching for the peace, security, and freedom of conscience which had been denied them in Schriesheim. Arriving in the cold of winter, Mack secured permission from Count Henry to purchase property in Wittgenstein, and was assured freedom of conscience by the tolerant count. Joyfully, Mack bought a house with land enough for a large garden. His new home was next to the path that led through the wooded hills from Schwarzenau to Berleburg.

The difficulties of the past year dimmed, to become in retrospect of little consequence as Mack welcomed new opportunities in a new land. He now participated with Hochmann in preaching missions, and may even have gone on some of his own. He invited other Separatists into his own home for Pietistic gatherings. He became acquainted with Separatists of varying theological perspectives who lived in Schwarzenau, and the enthusiasm and the stimulation of these contacts increased Mack's religious zeal. He had become convinced that one's highest loyalty belonged not to the Palatinate, nor to Schriesheim, nor to the Reformed Church, but to a living Christ whose word was revealed through the New Testament and through the Spirit within each believer.

Much had occurred in two short years, but there is no indication in any record to suggest that Alexander Mack harbored regrets over the pilgrimage he had begun, or foresaw the measure of its far-reaching effect.

CHAPTER V

A Time of Preparation
1706-1708

In the tranquility of rural Schwarzenau, Alexander Mack and his family found religious freedom and civil peace at last—striking contrast to what they had experienced in war-ridden and intolerant Schriesheim. In the lovely Eder River valley, the Macks discovered a community of mutual love and support, a community composed of Separatists and other religious nonconformists. By 1710 about three hundred religious dissenters had settled in or near this village. Although some of these refugees chose to live as hermits in the dense forests, most settled in the village or on the hillside overlooking Schwarzenau, living in tiny hastily constructed and rather flimsy huts. Mack, one of the few refugees who could afford a house, used his home for Pietistic gatherings.

Located between Marburg on the south and Kassel on the north, protected from main highways and marching armies by heavily wooded hills, Schwarzenau had not been so devastated by occupying troops as had Schriesheim. Its farmland, though, was not as fertile as the Rhine River plain of the Palatinate. Winding through the valley and the small village of Schwarzenau was the beautiful Eder River. By its banks the occasional flat areas and gentle slopes were used for growing crops or grazing cattle. Generally, however, the terrain was hilly, covered by dense forests which provided the primary economic resource of the area.

Spanning the Eder River in the center of Schwazenau was an ancient arching bridge, a stone bridge of simple beauty. To one side of this bridge stood a large manor house, a small castle in which members of the ruling family of Wittgenstein lived. To the other side stood a mill, where Mack may have occasionally worked. A cluster of small houses built close to the river were occupied by farmers, who went out to their fields early in the morning to till the soil, returning home at dusk.

Count Henry Albert (1658-1723) was the ruler of that section of Wittgenstein which included Schwarzenau. He was a religiously sensitive and tolerant ruler. During his entire reign, he welcomed refugees into his territory and encouraged them to settle there by leasing portions of his own land to them at moderate yearly fees. By cutting timber in the forests and farming the cleared land, these refugees could earn a rather meager and hardly adequate income. They preferred to accept lower wages rather than forego religious freedom for a better income elsewhere.

As long as these refugees were peaceable and relatively quiet about their faith, Count Henry was glad to have them live in Schwarzenau. Not only did they enhance his wealth by their work and presence, but Count Henry himself was sympathetic to many of their religious ideas. Four of his sisters had become Pietists, and had married commoners in spite of the disapproval of neighboring royalty. Schwarzenau was a genuine refuge and a haven of peace for the war-weary Rhinelanders.

By 1707, there were several different groups of Pietists living in Schwarzenau. The most enduring was the group which met in the home of Alexander and Anna Margaret Mack. This group met on Sunday afternoons or weekday evenings around the fireplace in Mack's "big room." A typical gathering included several families, one or two widows, and several unmarried persons—all searching together for the truth which they believed Jesus had taught. Services began with the singing of their favorite Pietistic hymns, followed by unison voicing of the Lord's Prayer. When Hochmann was present, he would stand before the group with his Bible in his hand to "explain the word"[1]—with great zeal in a loud voice. In Hochmann's absence, Mack would interpret the scripture. After the scriptural exposition, the whole group would kneel, raising high their arms in fervent prayer. Following a hymn and a closing prayer, the group would disperse.

During the spring and the summer of 1707, Mack and Hochmann traveled together to preach and give encouragement to Pietists living in other areas. Since many Pietists had fled to the Marienborn area northeast of Frankfurt, it is quite likely that they visited and preached there. The count of Ysenburg-Büdingen-Marienborn,

Charles August, was, like Count Henry of Wittgenstein, tolerant toward religious refugees, although he would not permit the establishment of any new religious organizations or the public practice of any deviant religious rites. These restrictions caused problems for the Brethren when they began to baptize adult converts.

Traveling farther, Mack and Hochmann would have received a warm welcome among the Pietists of Basel, Switzerland, a city on the Rhine River about sixty miles south of Heidelberg. There are no records to show that Mack visited old friends there, in the village of Frankendorf. However, if their visit was made in the late spring of 1707 they almost certainly visited the Boni brothers, Andrew and Martin, who were being severely tried and tested for their faith.

In his early twenties, Andrew Boni had settled with his bride in Heidelberg, where in 1702 he received the honorable title, "master weaver," and was accepted as a citizen of that city. It was in Heidelberg that Boni became an ardent Pietist and a close friend of both Alexander Mack and Martin Lucas.

Upon the death of his wife in 1705, Boni returned to Basel, where he enthusiastically proclaimed his new Pietistic beliefs. Unsympathetic, the local pastor complained to the civil authorities that Boni not only preached heresy but also refused to take the oath or appear at holy communion. To make matters even more strained, Boni refused to bear arms or participate in the regular drill required of all Swiss male citizens. When questioned, Boni denied none of the charges brought against him, but he promised that he would soon leave Basel.

Upon his return to Heidelberg in 1706, Boni resumed his Pietistic activities. But by August he was encountering the same kind of harassment that Mack and Hochmann were receiving in Schriesheim. Boni may well have attended the August 22, 1706, meeting in Schriesheim to hear Hochmann and Erb preach in the Mack mill. He also could have been one of their visitors at the prison in Mannheim.

When the Palatinate government outlawed Pietism on September 14, 1706, Boni returned to Basel. Unfortunately, neither Boni nor his beliefs were welcomed. The mayor expressed his concern to the town council that Andrew had influenced his brother Martin "and that Boni had met 'with a favorable response' among the common people."[2] Even Boni's parents strongly disapproved of his beliefs and actions.

Events moved rapidly toward an inevitable confrontation. On

November 21, 1706, Andrew was asked to appear as a sponsor at the baptism of his cousin's child. Since he opposed all military activity, Andrew appeared without the customary bayonet at his side and the bouquet in his hat which were worn by the Swiss men on such occasions.

After the service of baptism was complete, Boni asked the already-offended pastor where infant baptism was prescribed in the holy scriptures. Pulling out the New Testament which he carried with him at all times, Andrew pointed out that all biblical statements concerning baptism had to do with adults and that infants were incapable of understanding or participating in such ritual.

This scene so incensed Andrew's mother that on Monday following the baptism she went to the pastor to denounce her own son publicly. She told of the fierce arguments which had occurred in their home between father and son; but, since Andrew planned to leave Basel three weeks later, she asked the pastor not to present his case to the town council before his departure. By Friday, the pastor had reported the whole episode to the authorities and on Saturday Martin and Andrew Boni were imprisoned in Spalen-Tower.

A court of seven men cross-examined the two brothers, attempting to force them to name other Pietists in the Basel area. Both adamantly refused to divulge such information. By December 1, 1706, the interrogation was completed. Twelve days later the report of the local clergy concerning the Boni brothers' heresy was given to the city council. It listed explicitly the beliefs held by Andrew Boni, beliefs certainly held by many other Pietists, including Hochmann and Mack. Summarized and paraphrased, they are:

1. Infant baptism is totally rejected.
2. There should be no taking of oaths.
3. The church, composed of true Christians, should not tolerate blatant sinners.
4. There should be no force in religion.
5. The Christian can attain perfection through gradual growth.
6. A professional clergy is not biblically sanctioned, for any Christian who receives the gift of the Holy Spirit may rise up in a congregation to teach.[3]

The decision of the city council was that Martin Boni was to receive instruction from the Reformed clergy, but Andrew Boni was to be put in a pillory for a time and was then to be expelled forever from Basel, with immediate arrest to follow should he ever return.

When Boni was informed of the decision, he replied that he would "commend it to God," which the authorities understood as a promise to leave Basel and never return. But Boni had not accepted the punishment. He believed himself innocent of wrong-doing. So, on December 29, he wrote a letter to the mayor, defending his decision to stay in the Basel area, and explaining why he had not accepted his exile. The authorities wasted no time. On the same day that the letter was written and delivered, they notified all officers in the area to take Boni into custody. Relatives and friends were strictly forbidden to accept any of his letters.

Four months later, on April 22, 1707, the ruler at Waldenberg, a village twenty miles from Basel, apprehended Boni and sent him under custody back to Basel. In an eloquent letter, written from prison on April 27, 1707, and addressed to the city council, Boni called upon the whole city to repent, to "give themselves to God, and to renounce all that is worldly and temporal."[4] Boni's letter apparently made little impact upon the city council, for they ordered that he should be placed in the pillory again and then be "expelled forever under penalty of beating with switches."[5]

Although it is not certain when Mack and Hochmann visited Basel, if they were there while Andrew Boni was in prison they were possibly instrumental in relocating him in Schwarzenau. Sometime in 1707 or 1708, while living in Schwarzenau, Andrew married the widow Joanna Nöthiger. It is doubtful that he was ever reconciled with his estranged parents.

Another place on the Rhine River where Mack and Hochmann likely stopped was Strassburg. Here a number of Pietists had expressed views considered very extreme by the established church. Among these Pietists was Michael Eckerlin, a skilled tailor and cap maker, once a notable citizen of Strassburg and member of the city council. As early as 1701, Eckerlin had held Pietistic worship services in his home. The church officials, becoming quite agitated, denounced Eckerlin and others to the city government. After a series of investigations Eckerlin was found guilty in 1705, was led out of the city by guards armed with battle-axes, and was expelled forever from Strassburg. Eckerlin and his family also eventually found refuge in Schwarzenau, where they became part of the Baptist movement.

From 1609 to 1710, when the persecution against the Mennonites had reached its climax in Switzerland, a number of Swiss Mennonite refugees had settled in the Rhine valley.[6] Hochmann and

Mack visited some of the Anabaptist congregations. Mack respected the Mennonite emphasis on discipleship and community life. He found their pattern of adult baptism and disciplined community living more consonant with the scriptures than the highly individualistic and subjective faith of the Pietists.

Mack's son, Alexander, Jr., wrote that his father "visited in heartfelt love from time to time various meetings of the Mennonites in Germany."[7] It is reasonable to assume that some of these visits occurred during 1707 and early 1708 when Mack was developing his personal religious convictions in a way that would manifest itself as being quite independent of Hochmann. Mennonite life and faith may well have been powerful influences upon Mack at this stage of his spiritual development. Robert Friedman, a Mennonite historian, observed that when the Pietistic movement spread over Germany about 1700, Mennonites recognized some kinship to the movement and "opened their hearts and homes to this new message."[8] The hospitality extended to Mack and Hochmann exemplifies their increasing receptivity to the Pietistic spirit.

For Mack, baptism was a perplexing issue to which he must have given much thought during his travels. It was one thing to reject infant baptism as a perversion of scripture; it was quite another to determine what should take its place. Many Pietists and Quakers, and Hochmann himself, believed that sincerely repentant Christians were baptized through an emotionally charged conversion experience by the Holy Spirit. But as early as 1703, the question of baptism with water had arisen. Some of Hochmann's followers requested baptism according to the mode by which Jesus was baptized in the Jordan River. Although Hochmann was opposed to infant baptism, he did not believe at that time that any outer form of baptism was necessary.

Mack differed from Hochmann at this point. He was inclined to take seriously both the example of Christ and the direct command in Matthew 28 to baptize (immerse) disciples "into the name of the Father, and of the Son, and of the Holy Spirit."[9] It was only a question of time, upon his return to Schwarzenau, until Mack had to confront the problem of adult baptism by water.

As early as 1706, before Hochmann and Mack's long trip to various Pietistic centers, some of the Schwarzenau Separatists were convinced of their need for outer baptism. They had arrived at this conviction rather privately. When someone first dared to raise this question publicly, saying, "We must be baptized according to the teachings of Jesus Christ and the apostles,"[10] there was vigorous opposition. Like Hochmann, most of the Pietists had been disillusioned by "outward forms" and were quite content to enjoy their inner spiritual state. The question was not put to rest!

Sometime, perhaps in the late summer of 1707, Mack returned to Schwarzenau, feeling responsibility for his own family and the community of followers there. Hochmann, filled with a restless urge to proclaim the availability of God's love and forgiveness and human need for repentance, continued his preaching visits to other Pietistic gatherings.

The intensity of friendship, love, and commitment felt by the Schwarzenau Pietists for one another led to a functioning, if not formally organized, mutual aid or communitarian society. If anyone was in need, the others would provide concrete help. If someone was hungry, others would provide food. If a newcomer needed a hut for protection against the damp winter weather, others would join in building it.

Since Mack was the most prosperous of all the refugees, the financial burden resting upon him was unusually heavy. Therefore, he made arrangements to sell the last of his inheritance in Schriesheim, consummating the sales on January 23, February 5, and October 1, 1707. Some of these transactions may have been made by Mack while he was traveling in the Palatinate with Hochmann. If Mack did go to the Schriesheim area for the October 1 sale, he went alone, for Hochmann had gone to Nürnberg to visit the city of his childhood, where one of his two brothers lived.

Invited to Weissenbrunn by a Pietist group, Hochmann attended a Sunday service at which a young student in theology presided. After the reading of the Bible, Hochmann was invited to speak. The student was shocked at what Hochmann said! Later, while Hochmann was speaking to a group in an open field not far from Weissenbrunn, a burly local official seized him, manhandled him, and led him away. The civil authorities were so upset that a nobleman like Hochmann had been mistreated by a common local official that they promptly released him. Hochmann graciously forgave the fellow—after insisting that the man expressly apologize to him!

Another Pietistic gathering that Hochmann attended took place in the village of Leimburg. He spoke in a room filled with people, while fifty to sixty more stood outside. The following evening more than two hundred joined those outside the house, listening with no difficulty to the eloquent speech of the charismatic Hochmann.

Hochmann's speeches and popularity aroused much opposition, seriously embarrassing his second brother, an ambitious functionary of the royal court at Vienna. Apparently, it was this brother who instigated Hochmann's arrest and imprisonment in Nürnberg on October 12, 1707. Although the Nürnberg authorities were inclined to release Hochmann in a relatively short time, his brother prolonged his confinement for more than a year.

While in prison, Hochmann became a strong defender of freedom of conscience. On June 27, 1708, he wrote to the city council:

> I have petitioned the council for my freedom which has come to me as a noble and costly gift from God and nature. Please permit me, on account of conscience, to emigrate from here and to go to such places that tolerate the impartial truth as well as the spontaneous, sincere piety which consists of faith in God's Son and heartfelt love for one's brothers. Such faith has a sensitive conscience that will not in the least violate Divine and natural law, nor does it have the power to impinge on a conscience that is ruled by God, but rather has the courage to recognize that all public authorities are limited to promoting the public welfare and domestic tranquility. The purpose of all of this is that the consciences of men may be surrendered totally to Christ as the true shepherd of the sheep who alone knows how he shall bring his own to the true obedience of faith and love.[11]

Though the city council refused to release him, he was soon placed under house arrest in the care of his Viennese brother.

While Hochmann was imprisoned in Nürnberg struggling for his freedom, and while Mack was in Schwarzenau confronting the increasingly insistent question of baptism, the situation for Anna Margaret Mack's father, John Valentine Kling, was worsening in Schriesheim. Time had deepened the antagonism between Pastor Agricola and the Kling family. Finally, the rupture became irreparable. On December 8, 1707, the pastor and six elders formally excommunicated Kling and his wife from membership in the Schriesheim Reformed church.

A close friend of Mack, Martin Lucas, was also under surveillance. He was one of the leading Pietists in the Schriesheim-Heidelberg area. A buttonmaker by trade, a fellow prisoner with Hochmann and Erb at the Mannheim jail in September 1706, Lucas frequently held religious services in his own home. Occasionally he attended other Pietistic gatherings with John Valentine Kling. He no longer attended church services on Sunday mornings or participated in holy communion. Furthermore, he believed with all sincerity that even the "Turks and heathen" could be saved without baptism if they recognized Christ as Lord and truly repented of their sins. Born of Catholic parents in Bayonne, France, in 1651, Lucas was perhaps the oldest of those who became the early Brethren.

On Sunday morning, May 1, 1708, Lucas and John Valentine Kling, Mack's father-in-law, attended the Reformed church service in the village of Gross-Sachsen. The pastor of this church was friendly toward Pietistic thought and he invited the two men to his home for Sunday dinner. That evening, Lucas and Kling returned to the Kling home for supper, after which they participated in a Pietistic devotional service.

However, Herr Schumm, the same official from Heidelberg who had broken into the meeting at the Mack mill on August 22, 1706, heard about the service and sent his henchmen to break into this gathering; there they arrested Kling, Lucas, and two others. Schumm had even warned them of the government decree which outlawed Pietism, giving the arresting officers the right to imprison offenders, restrict their diet to bread and water, and put them to work with wheel-barrow and stone to build city fortifications. Schumm had the evidence against both Lucas and Kling. They had been caught in the act of studying the Bible, singing hymns, and praying their own prayers in a private group when the officers broke into their meeting.

On the following Thursday, Schumm preferred formal charges against them. On May 10, ten days after their arrest, the Heidelberg government fined the Pietists one hundred *Reichstaler,* a very heavy fine, imprisoned them, and gave them four weeks to join a legal church and refute Pietism.

Kling and Lucas appealed to the ecclesiastical authorities in Heidelberg. Within two weeks, on May 25, the consistory voted on the case, passing a resolution urging the government to set the prisoners free. Kling and Lucas, in addition, personally petitioned the government. They pointed out that they had been reared in the Reformed faith, had never separated from that faith, and were simply trying to enter more completely into the fellowship of the saints. As a result of their petitions, the prisoners were ordered to undergo an investigation to determine whether they were truly aligned with a legal church. If evidence supported such an alignment, they would be released on May 27.

Since the Pietists were drawn together by their adversities, they frequently wrote letters back and forth between families and communites. Alexander and Anna Margaret Mack were kept informed of the whole development. They felt no shame over Kling's imprisonment—it was simply a part of faithful crossbearing and was often considered an opportunity to grow in the faith. Yet, one did not rejoice in imprisonment *per se* or seek it needlessly. The prisons were dark, damp, miserable dungeons built beneath some castle or city wall—lice-infested, overrun by rodents, and smelling of human excrement. Sympathetic Pietists knew these conditions and did everything conscientiously possible to help bring about release. In Schwarzenau, Mack was in no position to give direct help. In Nürnberg, Hochmann, still in prison, sent a letter to the prisoners encouraging them to remain "composed in the Lord" through all their trials, assuring them that he was likewise remaining faithful to his calling.

The prisoners were finally released, but were required to submit to further intensive questioning. This new investigation began on June 8, 1708. In this hearing, Kling explained why he did not feel that he could return to the legal church at Schriesheim: (1) Pastor Agricola had attempted to persuade Kling to testify against his own son-in-law, Alexander Mack, and Kling had refused; (2) because of this refusal, Kling had been excommunicated from the church and dismissed from the town council; and (3) he was being charged unfairly simply because he had occasionally attended services in other Reformed churches.

The consistory was satisfied with Kling's sincerity and excused him upon the payment of his fine.

The investigation of Martin Lucas was more damaging. While in prison Lucas had written a letter to a prominent Pietist in Eppstein, Christian Liebe, sending greetings through him to his own "dear wife," and reporting that God had wrought a miracle while he had been in prayer. Lucas also mentioned that a hangman in Frankenthal had attended some of their meetings. Unfortunately, this letter was intercepted and used against Lucas at his hearing. Although Lucas was released after paying his fine, he was rearrested a year later and dealt with even more harshly.

These were the struggles and the beginnings: Hochmann in

prison wrestling with ideas about freedom and conscience; Mack in Schwarzenau struggling over issues of obedience to Christ in ritual and in Christian community; Kling and Lucas under investigation; and the continued widespread harassment of those Pietists who kept the faith.

The Eder River and valley, site of the Schwarzenau baptism.

CHAPTER VI

The Schwarzenau Baptismal Service
August 1708

By the spring of 1708 all the families who would be involved in the establishment of the New Baptists had arrived in Schwarzenau. During the spring and the summer all of them, and many other dissenters, had become deeply interested in the question of baptism, the issue that became the catalyst for creating a new denomination. But Hochmann, their leader, was still in prison at Nürnberg. It was scarcely an auspicious time to talk about establishing a religious community with group discipline, a new form of baptism, and a love feast service which would include feetwashing, a meal, and holy communion. Yet these were the issues which the Pietists in Schwarzenau were pondering in their hearts and discussing in their religious gatherings.

In the early summer of 1708 two "foreign brethren," most likely Collegiants from Holland, visited Schwarzenau. The Collegiants were a loosely organized Anabaptist group who baptized by immersion—a baptism in which the postulant knelt once forward. Resembling the Quakers in their informal services, and similar to the Mennonites in many of their other practices, they were well known for their piety and philanthropic activities. The two visitors strongly urged the Pietists in Schwarzenau to be baptized. Those who had been concerned about baptism had been loathe to speak about it publicly, since adult baptism was still punishable by death according to imperial law. With the arrival of the two "foreign brethren" the issue was finally brought into the open.

On July 4, Mack and another Schwarzenau Pietist carefully composed a letter to Hochmann at Nürnberg requesting his counsel concerning a service of baptism for adults. They also inquired about his views on the love feast.

Hochmann did not tarry in answering that letter. Writing from prison on July 24, 1708, he gave his approval of adult baptism if it followed true repentance and faith. He did not believe that baptism was essential, but if God were leading some of his children to be immersed in flowing water as Christ himself had been immersed, Hochmann would have no objection. He stressed that such a belief must be thoroughly tested to make sure it truly was from God, and soberly warned them of the possible consequences:

> From such actions at the present time will inevitably follow nothing but the cross and misery, as the anti-Christ will still rage against the members of Jesus Christ. One must, therefore, first carefully count the cost if one will follow after the Lord Jesus in all the trials which will certainly follow from this.[1]

Since the advocacy of adult baptism was itself illegal and easily subject to misunderstanding by his Separatist friends, Hochmann asked that only those who can "bear and understand it be given the letter to read."[2]

So far as the love feast was concerned, his opinion was the same as for baptism. It must be based on the love of Jesus and on an appropriate community of faithful members.

When they received this letter in the first week of August 1708, the little band of Pietists rejoiced, for they believed that Hochmann had unreservedly approved their plans. Looking to him as their spiritual adviser, they expected that upon his release from prison he would join them in their fellowship.

In their enthusiasm they decided to choose by lot one person from their group to draft a letter inviting the religious dissenters in and near Schwarzenau to participate in "this high act of baptism."[3]

The letter was written. The author remained unknown. Three basic reasons were given for baptism by adult immersion: (1) the example of Christ's baptism in the Jordan River; (2) the commandment of Jesus in Matthew 28 to "make disciples of all peoples, baptizing them in the name of the Father, and of the Son, and of the Holy Spirit"; (3) the example of the early church. It was made quite clear that baptism in and of itself was not essential for salvation. It allowed for that person, "grounded in God," who did not consider water baptism necessary, to live conscientiously "according to his or her own calling." The letter closed with a forceful plea for others to join the pending baptismal service.

There were many reasons for holding a baptismal service. It is quite clear that some of those involved in its planning wanted to establish a *Gemeinde,* a community or congregation. Considerable discussion—and dissatisfaction—had developed because there was no structure to implement some of the clear teachings of the scripture. They were distressed that there was no church to go to for help as Matthew 18 advised members to do in case of serious dispute. The lack of churchly structure made them feel very insecure.

Other Pietists were anxious about their personal salvation. They no longer believed in infant baptism, yet there was no believers' baptism to take its place. Was this lack of ritual not a violation of the New Testament directive to be baptized? For them, this was a very real concern.

Some Pietists were not interested in helping to start a new denomination. Dismayed by controversies among competing Pietistic leaders and discouraged by excessive individualism and lack of stable guidelines, they returned to the established church from which they had come. Most of the Pietists in the area, however, were satisfied with their own religious condition and did not respond to the baptismal letter.

Mack, and others in his group, felt called by God to be a separate people, and decided to proceed with a public baptismal service. There was no doubt in Mack's mind that infant baptism had no validity. Nor was there any doubt in his mind about the need for a "believers' baptism" to be by immersion. The scholarly works of Gottfried Arnold, with which Mack was clearly familiar, showed that immersion was the apostolic practice, performed in flowing water.

Yet one pressing problem remained, one which had to be settled before the baptismal service was performed. What posture or mode should be used? Should the applicants recline, to be immersed once backwards, as the English Baptists did? Should they bow once forward as the Dutch Collegiants did? Or was there still a different way?

Mack could not find explicit instructions in the New Testament; but, by consulting Gottfried Arnold's books and other books on church history, he found some indication that the early church had immersed the whole body three times forward in harmony with the Trinitarian formula. Mack became convinced that trine immersion had been the common practice of the early and medieval church, abbreviated in the course of time to the pouring or sprinkling patterns used in the established churches.

After much Bible study, prayer, and discussion, eight individuals decided to risk all they had gained of tranquility and peace in Schwarzenau in exchange for immersion in the flowing water of the Eder. Plans were made. The service was to be held not far from the stone bridge at the center of the village, sometime between August 5 and August 8.[4] The date was never recorded, a precaution taken to preserve its secrecy. Pietists were generally opposed to holy days and they hoped to protect this day from becoming one. The service was to be held very early in the morning—perhaps at dawn—when few of the townspeople would be awake.

At the designated time eight persons gathered at the bank of the river to establish, in Alexander Mack, Jr.'s, words, "a covenant of good conscience with God."[5] Anna Margaret Mack stood beside her husband, Alexander, the recognized leader of the group, in charge of the service. Andrew Boni, from Basel, estranged from his parents and unable to write openly to his brother, Martin, was there with Joanna, his bride of less than a year. George Grebe, a former gunsmith, was also present. Grebe had been the court gunsmith to the government in Kassel, the largest city in Hesse. As early as 1700, Grebe had welcomed itinerant Pietists into his home. When the government of Hesse, like the government of Palatinate, sought to repress Pietism in 1706, Grebe and his wife fled from Kassel to Schwarzenau. Luke Vetter also stood on the bank of the Eder that historic morning. Like Grebe, Vetter and his wife had fled to Schwarzenau from Hesse. Completing the list of the original eight were John and Joanna Kipping. Unlike the others, who had all been reared in the Reformed faith, the Kippings had been Lutheran, drawn to Pietism, perhaps, by the active Pietistic movement within their church at Württemberg.

The group wanted Mack to baptize them, but he refused to perform the first baptism because he himself had not been baptized by immersion. The other four men then cast lots to choose one who would baptize Mack. There was common agreement among them that his name would never be revealed.[6]

After singing several Pietistic hymns, and reading the portion from Luke 14 about "counting the cost" (as Hochmann had suggested), the anonymous officiant waded into the clear cold water of the Eder with Mack. Kneeling in the water, Mack responded affirmatively to the baptismal vows, then bowed his head and body under the water in three distinct acts of total immersion as his brother in the faith baptized him into "the name of the Father, and of the Son, and of the Holy Spirit."

Following a prayer of forgiveness and blessing, Mack humbly baptized the one who had baptized him. Then he baptized the other three men and three women. Following the baptisms the group sang a favorite hymn, received a benedictory blessing, and solemnly dispersed, transported by religious zeal, confident that what they had done was approved by God even though not by the government. Some time later Mack composed a hymn entitled "Count Well the Cost," reflecting the agony, the risk, and the tension as well as the joy and deep religious satisfaction surrounding this baptismal service. Two of the thirteen stanzas proclaim:

> Christ Jesus says, "Count well the cost
> When you lay the foundation."
> Are you resolved, though all seem lost,
> To risk your reputation,
> Your self, your wealth, for Christ the Lord
> As you now give your solemn word?
>
> Into Christ's death you're buried now
> Through baptism's joyous union.
> No claim of self dare you allow
> If you desire communion
> With Christ's true church, His willing bride,
> Which, through His Word, He has supplied.[7]

These eight newly immersed Christians felt that now, in reality, they had a "covenant of good conscience with God."

No longer Separatists, individuals, a miscellaneous collection of Christians, disenchanted with established religion, they were now a *Gemeinde,* a congregation, a church, the "New Baptists" or "Schwarzenau Baptists," as they called themselves. Even though they did not like to think of themselves as founding a new denomination, by their action that is exactly what they did, and very soon they began to view themselves as a distinct church, separate from the other churches of Christendom.

Caught up in the rebirth of their faith, and supported in their zeal by a commonly shared religious experience, they became quite certain that their small church was a very real part of the church of Christ; and that the established Reformed, Lutheran, and Catholic churches had sadly forsaken the true faith of the New Testament, and could scarcely be considered a part of the true church of Christ.

Although the transcendent joy of this first baptismal service sustained and encouraged Mack, two shadows dimmed his jubilant celebration. The group had violated imperial law, and no one could predict the result. Moreover, he was quite aware that many of his closest and dearest friends did not approve of his action. What effect would this have on their spirit of community?

Strong in his faith, however, Mack was so firmly convinced of the virtue and rightness of what he had done that he felt himself ready to accept whatever persecution might come. During the days which followed, the heavy responsibility for providing leadership and spiritual encouragement lay upon his shoulders. A new era had begun for the New Baptists of Schwarzenau.

CHAPTER VII

The Community of New Baptists
August-December 1708

Within a few days, news of the Schwarzenau baptismal event spread to many other Pietistic groups, from Kassel in the north to Schriesheim in the south, from Krefeld in the west to Marienborn in the east. Comparisons of this new German religious community, the New Baptists of Schwarzenau, were made to its English counterpart across the channel, the British Baptists, and to the Collegiants in Holland. Many received the news with great interest, some with marked disapproval.

As early as August 11, J. A. Haller, a theological student at the University of Heidelberg and friend of Martin Lucas, heard about the baptism. Immediately, he wrote to John George Gichtel, a venerable patriarch among the Pietists, seventy years old, and a follower of the mystic, Jacob Böhme.[1] Gichtel gave close attention to all developments in Schwarzenau from his home in Amsterdam. He did not approve of them. On December 10, he replied to the student in Heidelberg, expressing his opinion that physical water was insufficient; true baptism must be in the water of eternal life which only Christ can supply:

> The good souls in Schwarzenau, who have themselves baptized in the natural water, are not deeply enough grounded. . . . Time will reveal their error to them.[2]

Gichtel's views were undoubtedly echoed by many other Separatists. They looked with suspicion upon any attempt to create yet another denomination with new legalistic forms and inevitable hypocrisy. Mack knew of such criticisms, but he had never been strongly attracted by either the mysticism of Böhme or the separatistic individualism of Gichtel. He was probably not seriously disturbed by such criticism, for he was involved in weightier matters.

A more disappointing development came from Hochmann. Though Mack was the recognized minister of the New Baptists, Hochmann was still considered their true spiritual leader. They looked forward with great anticipation to his release from prison and his return to Schwarzenau to join their fellowship. This dream was never realized.

When Hochmann was finally released from prison, he traveled to the Marienborn area to visit friends. Here he was told for the first time about the baptismal service in Schwarzenau and the subsequent reactions. News of the event had also reached Count Friedrich Ernest von Solms in Laubach, a sympathetic nobleman with whom Hochmann had voluminous correspondence. The count wrote to Hochmann asking for his opinion on the matter.

On November 2, Hochmann wrote from the home of Christian Erb, his former prison companion in Mannheim, observing that nothing can "truly change the person except when Jesus himself baptizes the innermost depths of the heart with fire, and with the Holy Spirit."[3] He conceded that those who desired baptism by immersion should have that freedom and not be persecuted for it. However, Hochmann upheld love as the expression of faith which must rule in every aspect of one's life and practice. In Christianity, he could find no place for determining that a believer must do this or not do that. Instead, everything must be left to Christian freedom under the discipline of love—even the question of public, adult baptism: "The freedom of Christ suffers neither force nor laws."[4]

A few days later, Christian Liebe of Eppstein likewise turned to Hochmann for counsel about these baptisms, which had become a real concern for many believers. Hochmann's reply was much the same as the one he had sent to Count Friedrich Ernest. To Liebe he added a word of caution: "I want to advise warmly, however, that they do not begin a sectarian spirit against others who are not inwardly impelled to the outward baptism."[5]

Thus a significant difference became apparent between Mack's and Hochmann's beliefs. Hochmann saw baptism as a valid but not necessary expression of one's inner faith experience. For Mack, faith impelled one to follow Christ's example unreservedly. For Mack, baptism was a necessary symbol of Christian faith-obedience.

As the new church developed, the group looked to Alexander

Mack as its minister and *Vorsteher,* "elder-in-charge." Since they believed in divine ordination of ministers by the Holy Spirit, there was probably no formal election or acknowledgement of Mack's position. Neither he nor the group wanted to recognize anybody as the "founder" of the church. Their interpretation was that the New Baptist fellowship had been established by a group decision, and that the true founder was Jesus. In its origin as a church, Mack was considered its inspirational leader rather than its founder.

Mack's spiritual pilgrimage began with his confirmation in the Reformed church of Schriesheim. Unmoved by traditional religious forms, he was aroused by the simple but profound spiritual dedication of the Pietists to develop his own personal devotional life. For about two years he broke completely away from the church, becoming a Separatist with no institutional religious affliation. Finally, in 1708, he found himself unquestionably established as the leader of a free Baptist congregation in Schwarzenau, far from the home of his childhood.

Mack did not have the monumental or dominating ego characteristic of many religious leaders. Of genuine humility, his religious quest was an expression of his sincere opening to new knowledge, experiences, and possibilities. When he broke away from the established church, he broke forever with the view that religious truth is a closed system. In the formation of the small Baptist congregation, he rejected, however, the view that religious truth is solely the responsibility of each individual. In his isolation from the church, separated from members of his family and friends, he became more and more convinced that community was essential to faith and to helping the individual make decisions in harmony with the will of God.

Following the baptismal service, the group, under Mack's leadership, made many decisions about the nature of their community, planned for propagating their faith, and developed a clear sense of their own identity. As they formulated their policies and doctrines, the new Baptists developed a view of the New Testament church as their model for the life of the congregation, an idea they shared with the Mennonites. They were not interested in literally reproducing specific features of the apostolic church, but in following New Testament guidelines for congregational life and practice. They were definitely not interested in imitating existing churches. Mack specifically stated that they had neither a new church nor new laws.

In this respect, they were quite similar to many other Protestant denominations which in their beginnings claimed to be recovering the true nature of the apostolic church.

The New Baptists met for worship in the evening, choosing not to meet on Sunday morning lest they become like the legal, apostate churches. In their services, no traditional creeds were used. Creeds were considered to be "of man rather than God" and to be deterrents to new light breaking forth from the Word. Quite different from the formality of traditional church services, their meetings were much more pentecostal in nature, but without *glossolalia* (speaking in tongues). Always kneeling for prayer, every member was free to participate. Some of the more ardent members prayed with such fervor that Gichtel complained that their prayer was so loud that "one's ears hurt."[6] Their singing was lusty as well. Using Freylinghausen's *Spiritual Songbook,*[7] they sang with great enthusiasm the Pietistic hymns with which they had become very familiar.

For interpreting scripture, Mack used Martin Luther's translation of the Bible. He was not a gifted speaker like Hochmann, but what he said was substantial and persuasive. Though not formally well educated, he was very familiar with the Bible and with Anabaptist and Pietist literature. He considered the guidance of the "Word" and the inner "promptings of the Spirit" as the ultimate sources of authority.

Mack had no need to defend God's existence, the holy Trinity, or the role of Christ's life in salvation. The New Baptists accepted the historic Christian faith and the basic principles of the Reformation. There probably was not an atheist within thirty miles of Schwarzenau.

The debt the New Baptists owed to the Reformation was well illustrated by the attitude of six members from Solingen who were imprisoned at Düsseldorf and Jülich between 1717 and 1720. When questioned by the authorities, they admitted to differing with the Heidelberg catechism on only three issues: baptism, the taking of oaths, and justification by faith.

Like the major Reformation leaders, Mack accepted the priesthood of all believers, in which each person takes responsibility for his own religious destiny. Mack felt that there was no need for a human mediator between the individual and God. With John Calvin, he rejected much of the practice of Catholicism, including the hierarchy of priests, the formality of the Mass, the papacy, and the veneration of the Virgin Mary. He could not accept the sale of indulgences for special merit, or the use of confession as a means for securing God's grace. Mack simply could not accept the authority of Catholic tradition or tolerate the scholastic philosophy of the Church Fathers.

Along with Luther and Calvin, Mack accepted the "direct" authority of the scriptures. He modified this concept, though, by teaching that only the New Covenant was binding upon the Christian. The Old Testament (Covenant), to Mack, was subordinate to the New, a prefiguration of the New Covenant in Christ Jesus.

Mack was, however, quite critical of several aspects of Reformation theology and practice. Because he viewed the Reformation through the eyes of Arndt, Spener, Francke, Arnold, and others it was impossible for him to accept the teachings of the Reformers *in toto*.

Mack believed so strongly in human freedom that he was not able, in any degree, to accept John Calvin's doctrine of predestination. For Mack, every individual was truly free to accept or reject the proffered gift of God in Jesus. He did not feel the need to argue this point; he simply assumed it.

The most radical deviation Mack made from Reformation theology was his repudiation of Luther's "justification of faith alone." Mack did not depreciate the importance of faith in salvation, but he clearly believed that more than faith was involved. He rejected the view that faith was an intellectual acceptance of propositional truth, a mere subscription to given creeds. Faith was, rather, a free response to the mysterious intervention of God's Spirit in one's own being. Faith was a trusting willingness to live in obedience to the pattern set by Christ.

There are places in Mack's writings where his emphasis on obedience seems to make of Jesus' teachings simply another Mosaic code filled with all the legalistic casuistry from which Jesus had joyously delivered his disciples. This emphasis on legalism is expressed in a paragraph from *Rights and Ordinances:*

> Note well how true believers in, and lovers of, the Lord Jesus always look steadfastly and singlemindedly to their Lord and Master in all things. They follow and obey him in all his commands, which he has told them to do, and has shown them by his own example.[8]

At other times, however, Mack viewed obedience not as submission to an authoritarian set of rules, but as a dynamic relationship to a transcendent vision. In following Christ, one does not destroy one's own will or spirit, but consciously redirects it in a new way out of a sincere love for Christ. According to Mack, the true follower of Christ must

> . . . cling to Jesus the Head as a true member in faith and love. He must be ready to give his body, and even life, unto death, if it is demanded of him, for the sake of Jesus and his teachings . . . .[9]

To these early Baptists, faith which was not experienced as an inner commitment to Christ and expressed in practical acts in everyday life was an invalid faith. Only through faith-obedience, expressed voluntarily through acts of love, is one ever made whole.

For the Reformers, salvation was an objective act of God. For Mack, salvation was strongly subjective with great emphasis placed upon the centrality of love in the inner being. Love, to Mack, was rooted in one's relationship with God, which flowered in loving relationships with others. The ultimate religious experience to this sensitive man was the experience of God's loving, healing, Holy Spirit manifested in love and concern for those in the community of faith and in compassion even for one's enemies. Mack's understanding of salvation was clearly Pietistic.

Mack's interpretation of faith was not only in terms of obedience, but was also like that of a growing plant rather than a finished structure. He could never accept creedal statements as definitive or systematic theologies as final. His sermons were designed to encourage his congregation in their struggle to grow in love, purity, and grace, "in favor with God and man." With other Pietists, Mack believed strongly in the Christian life as one of growth and openness. He recognized the possibility of a person's regeneration "to a considerable extent even before his baptism in water."[10]

This view of religion as process was almost unique. Francke had taught that conversion must take place at a specific instant. Mack saw conversion as a gradual process leading to a conscious moment of decision. Mack believed that Christians could attain perfection, but admitted humbly that he was far from that goal.

Mack's most overt disagreement with the Reformation was over the rite of baptism. In fostering the concept of the church as a voluntary, disciplined community, Mack openly and flagrantly rejected infant baptism.

Against infant baptism Mack could wax quite eloquent. Because of infant baptism, he claimed, Christians "go publicly to war and slaughter one another by the thousands."[11] Because babies automatically became Christian at baptism, he felt that the established churches failed to demand ethical responsibility on the part of their adult members. Remembering the pains of his childhood, Mack was "scandalized" by the "horrible wickedness" of Lutherans, Reformed, and Catholics—all of whom practiced infant baptism and yet helped to pillage the village of Schriesheim time after time. In believers' baptism, Mack believed, the Christian makes a mature and responsible decision to give one's self to a new way of life opposed to violence, destruction, and war.

Another fundamental difference which Mack had with the Reformation was over the nature of the church. In defining the church as a disciplined, voluntary community modeled after the New Testament church, Mack was following the pattern of the Mennonites. If the Mennonites had practiced immersion, Mack might well have joined forces with them, for he regarded their faith and life very highly.

Biblically, one of the most distinguishing marks of the New Testament church was its celebration of the Lord's Supper. Leading the New Baptists in a careful study of the scriptures, Mack developed a pattern for their love feast which has remained essentially unchanged to this day, including an examination service, feetwashing, a meal, and the bread and the wine.

In Schwarzenau the small band of members would gather in Mack's "big room" for a service of examination and praise, the men sitting around one table, the women around another. Only those Christians who had been immersed participated—those who had "separated themselves from the body of Satan, the world, yes, from all unrighteousness and from all false sects and religions."[12] The examination service was taken very seriously; so if a person felt himself unworthy, he would withdraw from participation.

Many of the Separatists looked upon this exclusiveness as proof that the New Baptists had indeed developed a highly sectarian spirit. But Mack's concern was to make the love feast a deeply spiritual and significant event in the lives of his people. Shocked by the practice of communion as he knew it in the established churches, he wrote that the church members there "do receive a bit of bread and a little wine, but at the same time are filled with great extravagance of

clothes, sensual debauchery, selfish pride, and the like."[13] Mack
believed that "obvious sinners," even if immersed, should not be permitted at the Lord's Supper.

In spite of such judgmental restrictions, or perhaps even because
of them, the spirit of the service was very joyous as they read from
the scriptures and sang hymns, some composed by one of them, as
was this one:

> This night we come intending
> Our minds to purify,
> Our lips Thy praise attending,
> Our hearts to sanctify.
> Now meet we with accord
> Our hearts to blend in singing,
> Thy goodness ever praising
> Here at Thy table, Lord.[14]

After the examination service, one of the ministers would read
from John 13 the story of Jesus' washing of the disciples' feet. At the
close of this reading, each man in turn would gird himself with a
towel and kneel to wash the feet of another as a symbol of true
humility and spiritual cleansing. The sisters did likewise. As the
feetwashing progressed, the group sang appropriate hymns, some
written just for the occasion, such as the following:

> How pleasant is it and how good
> That those who live as brothers should
> In faith and love uniting,
> Like servants wash each other's feet
> When at the feast of love they meet,
> In fellowship delighting.[15]

The group then ate quietly a simple meal of bread, broth and
beef, feeling a spirit of unity against the forces of evil which had long
plagued their lives. The intensity of the experience was heightened by
the gathering dusk, the cries of the night birds, and the solemnity of
the ritual. When they had finished, prayers of gratitude for the meal
and for life itself were given.

This dramatic reenactment of the last supper before Christ's
crucifixion was concluded with the Eucharist. After reading the account of Jesus' trial and crucifixion, Mack took the unleavened bread
in his hands and blessed it. He then broke a piece to give to his
neighbor, saying, "The bread which we break is the communion of

the body of Christ." Each participant did the same.

Mack then took the goblet of wine, praying God's blessing upon it also. He offered it to his neighbor, saying, "This cup which we drink is the communion of the blood of Christ." The cup was then passed to all present, with Mack taking the last sip.

Prayers of gratitude were again offered. A closing hymn was sung—perhaps the following, composed by one of the group:

> This night Thy bread we've broken;
> The cup we too have shared;
> Thus Thou to us have spoken,
> For whom Thy soul has cared.
> In faith to break this bread
> Christ's children it will strengthen;
> The chords of love will lengthen
> As in His path we tread.[16]

Mack then dismissed them with a benediction, after which all those present helped to clear up the disorder before returning to their homes.

In trying to pattern their congregational life after the style of the New Testament church, the new Baptists had to deal with many issues, not the least of which was the governance of the congregation. As a matter of principle Mack believed in a kind of democratic equality in which the final decision-making power rested in the congregation. He understood himself as ordained to provide spiritual leadership, not to rule the church. He did not believe there was any more reason for him to be paid than for those who led the group through eloquent prayers. He accepted no salary.

The group had to clarify its position with respect to the secular government. Mack's own attitude was somewhat mixed. Although he had violated the law of the Palatinate when he sponsored Pietistic gatherings in Schriesheim and again when he performed illegal baptisms in Schwarzenau, he was by no means antigovernment. He was quite willing to pay appropriate taxes and to give honor to the authorities in control, for, as he pointed out, "they are ordained of God to punish the evil and to help protect the good, provided they carry out their offices in accordance with the will of God."[17] In Mack's view, a Christian obeys civil law unless it clearly violates the higher law of God.

Yet another issue was that of oaths, which were demanded by the government on numerous occasions. Mack took the same position held by the Mennonites that Jesus had clearly taught his followers that the simple truth is sufficient.

> . . . Swear not at all; neither by heaven; for it is God's throne: Nor by the earth; for it is his footstool. . . . But let your communication be, Yea, yea; Nay, nay: for whatsoever is more than these cometh of evil.[18]

Perhaps the most controversial issue among the brothers and sisters was over sexual practices. The New Baptists believed that their faith demanded a whole new style of living, distinct and apart from the ways of the world. When the congregation was first organized, in its zeal to follow the example of Jesus its members practiced continence, even for those who were married. Mack admitted in 1713 that they had at first "rejected the married state."[19] The author of the *Ephrata Chronicle,* published in 1786, wrote that for seven years following their first baptismal service, the Brethren practiced continence.

The times were in ferment. Many different groups were experimenting with various life-styles. In a religious community established at Sassmanshausen, a few miles from Schwarzenau, by "Mother" Eva von Buttlar (1670-1721), a very different view of sex was taken. "Mother Eva," a very mystical and "pious" woman, attracted a rather large following. Setting herself up as the "Holy Spirit," she taught her followers that the lust of the flesh, spoken of in the Bible, could be purged only through a sexual relationship with a holy woman such as herself.

The New Baptists must certainly have been acquainted with this phenomenon. They established as their pattern of living a quite different style: no sexual experience, even with marriage partners.

The *Ephrata Chronicle* intimates that these New Baptists even established a mode of living in which husbands and wives lived separately from each other, as members of the Ephrata Cloisters later lived in Pennsylvania. However, the recorded experience of Lady Clara Elizabeth Callenberg, a Pietist from Kassel, refutes this suggestion. Turning away from life as she had known it, Lady Callenberg had chosen to live a life of poverty and complete dedication to God. She traveled to Schwarzenau, where she was given shelter by George Grebe and his wife, Clara. Lady Callenberg had known Grebe when he was a well-to-do gunsmith in Kassel. Now, as one of the original eight, he kindly showed mercy to her, permitting her to sleep in the attic under their roof for three weeks, "where she climbed every night like a hen."[20] In writing of her trip to Schwarzenau in 1709, Lady Callenberg reported that Grebe and his wife lived together in a small one-room hut.

It is apparent that the New Baptist couples continued to live together, but as brothers and sisters rather than as husbands and wives, attempting to be true to their conception of the New Testament ideal, and to the teachings of Arnold and Hochmann.

Arnold expressed his views in *The Marital and Celibate Lives of the First Christians,* a monumental volume divided into eight books. The fourth book was titled "Concerning the Obligations and the Behavior of the Early Christians Toward One Another." This book is further divided into twelve chapters, the fifth of which was titled "Concerning Chastity Among the Early Christians." In this chapter Arnold contends that many of the early Christians chose to remain single in order to follow Christ with single-minded devotion, following the advice of Saint Paul that in the light of the present distress people should not even look for wives and husbands.

In Arnold's view, even more to be praised than those who do not marry are those who, though married, practice continence. Arnold tells the story of a young Christian who was forced to marry against his will. After the marriage he and his bride chose to repudiate the ways of the world together, and to live as brother and sister.

Hochmann essentially agreed with Arnold. In his writing he illustrated five levels of male-female relationships. The lowest level is purely physical, such as a relationship with a prostitute. The next level was that of an honorable, respectable marriage, but one which had not been sanctified by true Christian commitment and salvation.

The third level was the Christian marriage in which "two souls who have been blessed through the blood of Christ are united by God's Spirit in marital love."[21] In such a marriage, according to Hochmann, the sexual relationship was primarily for procreation.

The fourth level, wrote Hochmann,

> . . . and yet much more nearly perfect grade of marriage is the continent marriage, where two persons who are absorbed in love for God and the Lamb live together with the purest kind of devotion to Christ. They are bound together in no other purpose than to serve God in Christ without interruption.[22]

In the fifth and highest level, the most nearly perfect level of all, the human soul loves only God. This is the level of pure, un-adulterated devotion to Christ. For such a person, the only progeny ever desired are the children in the faith who need encouragement and help. This is the pattern of life Hochmann chose for himself, and the model he urged the unmarried Pietists to choose for their future.

It is reasonable to infer that Mack and the early Baptist Brethren attempted to institute the fourth level of relationship as their pattern, but apparently without success. Mack admitted in some of his writings that difficulties had arisen over this question.

The *Ephrata Chronicle* was clearly in error when it estimated the Baptist period of continence as seven years, for Alexander Mack, Jr., was born on January 25, 1712, three years and five months after the Schwarzenau baptisms. At most, the period of continence must not have exceeded two and one-half years.

Whatever their reasons for surrendering continence in marriage, Mack and the New Baptists did not challenge Hochmann's high regard for celibacy as a Christian way of life. In *Rights and Or-dinances,* which Mack published in 1715, he wrote:

> If the unmarried state is conducted in purity of the spirit, and of the flesh, in true faith in Jesus, and is kept in true humility, it is better and higher than the married state. It is also closer to the image of Christ to remain unmarried.[23]

The New Baptists, reluctantly relinquishing continence, shifted deliberately to level three, and to the open advocacy of Christian marriage as an acceptable but not preferred pattern for Christian living. Mack admitted that

> . . . if an unmarried person marries, he commits no sin, provided it oc-curs in the Lord Jesus, and is performed in the true belief of Jesus Christ.[24]

Although a believer was not to marry an unbeliever, the most impor-tant test of the foundation for marriage was whether the partners treated each other respectfully with Christian love. If they did not, if one was "a wolf or a brute," there was no marriage relationship, ac-cording to Mack, and separation was permissible. "The believer should definitely not be bound to remain with such a vicious per-son."[25] To Mack, marriage without respect and caring, without com-mitted Christian love was not marriage at all but a prostitution of the marriage relationship.

These early Baptists were not more puritanical than the Mennonites or other Pietistic groups. They did not consider pleasure and sexual experience as sinful in themselves, but as being good only as they found their appropriate place in reference to the higher priorities of faithful obedience to God's divine will as revealed in Jesus Christ. Mack, at his best, was not an authoritarian, dogmatic legalist. He was open to alternatives which were explored by the faith community. He accepted group consensus. With sincerity and devotion to one another and to God, this little community came to the conclusion that a Christian marriage could include a sexual relationship within the context of Christian love.

It is apparent that the New Baptists, in their early experimental ventures, established some form of equalitarian, primitive communism patterned after the New Testament church as it was described in the book of Acts.[26] They refrain not only from sex for a time, but also from regular work. In the community all persons were equal and all possessions were shared in common. Women were on the same plane of equality as men, able to speak and pray publicly without restraint. In establishing such a community, the New Baptists emulated Hochmann's earlier experiment in communal living, which he called a *Laboratorium*.

In 1703 or early 1704, Hochmann wrote from Schwarzenau to a friend describing his *Laboratorium:*

> We do not consider a book-keeper as necessary, for Christ alone is our accountant, to whom we have given all our goods . . . . We are in this fellowship all equal and regard everyone as brother and sister . . . . Our sole government is the love of Christ which compels us to arrange our lives in loving service. Nobody is forced into formalized and constant work, for that is under the curse, and not appropriate to the fellowship of Christ.[27]

Hochmann further explains the communal commitment. He felt that in order to dedicate himself totally to Christ and a Christlike life he must sever all human connections. He asked for and received a severance of loyalty and obligation to his home principality of Nürnberg so that he could give of himself unreservedly to the "new community," whose purpose was to proclaim God's Kingdom as it was revealing itself in a new and radical way on earth. Like the organization of the New Baptists, Hochmann's *Laboratorium* was more than a self-serving organization.

Considering the period of history in which these events occurred, and the culture from which they grew, it is not surprising that this New Baptist experiment attracted more attention than its size seemed to warrant. Count Charles Louis, brother-in-law of the count who ruled Schwarzenau, denounced these dissenters for discarding "respect of wives for husbands and considerations for the family."[28] Other accusations cast at them were focused on their refusal to attend church, holding private meetings instead, where male and female alike were "permitted to teach and speak whatever the Spirit moves them to."[29] The count was probably more disturbed by the fact that women were allowed to speak in the services equally with men than he was over the fact that they were guided by the Spirit.

In their earliest years, the New Baptists did not make an ecclesiastical distinction between male and female. Sometime between 1708 and 1719, Alexander Mack ordained both Jacob Schröder and his wife as ministers. Upon the death of her husband, *Frau* Schröder continued as a minister in the church.[30]

The celibate, communal community did not continue long. After much controversy and discussion, both celibacy and a communal economy were rejected and more traditional patterns of living were reinstated. In a public debate, Mack claimed that certain leaders of the Pietistic movement—undoubtedly Arnold and Hochmann—had influenced him and the early Baptists to practice continence and communal living. "Before our baptism, when we were still with the Pietists," he wrote, "we were not taught otherwise by those who were deemed great saints."[31] Mack confessed that the New Baptists had much "contention" until they abandoned these "errors" which they had absorbed.

Like the Mennonites, Mack foresaw correctly that some kind of discipline was needed in order to preserve order within the community. The biblical basis for such discipline was Matthew 18:15-17, a procedure used by the Mennonites to return the wayward sinner to the fold. This procedure was called "the ban." If a member sinned openly and was not reconciled with the person sinned against, he was visited by the elders of the church and called upon to turn from his wicked ways and repent. If the "sinner" still did not repent, he was ordered to appear before the congregation. This was his final opportunity. If he still refused to confess his sin and repent, the congregation could pronounce the ban, after which all social relationships with the offender were suspended until he was willing to seek forgiveness through repentance. If the ban failed, excommunication followed.

Mack understood the ban, not as punishment—for only God can punish—but as a disciplinary act directed toward the restoration of full fellowship between the individual and the church. The practical consequences of the ban, though, were extensive. The sinner was ostracized from the life of the congregation. No one would engage him in friendly conversation. Members would not invite him into their homes. The most painful aspect of banning emerged in marriage. The wife had to participate just as fully in the ban as any other member of the congregation did. She could not talk to him, sleep with him, or express affection for him in any way.

The ban illustrates clearly the depth of commitment and the priority of God's will which these early Baptists felt. For them it was far better to suffer the temporary consequences of banning than to be separated from communion with God.

The ban did not proscribe acts of compassion. If a banned member needed food, or shelter, the congregation met that need with kindness. If sickness occurred, the family or the congregation cared for the offending member and his family. The ban was never to be practiced spitefully or harshly, but with deep concern and compassion for the spiritual healing and the forgiveness of the sinner.

From many sources, it becomes quite clear that the New Baptists were deeply spiritual, filled with caring concern for one another. The daughter of Count Henry, who probably lived in the Manor House at Schwarzenau, described them as a quiet people who "spend their time in Bible study, in prayer, and in deeds of kindness and charity."[32] Count Henry called them inoffensive "out of pure desire to lead lives pleasing to God."[33]

Their quiet nonresistance, or pacifism, was another feature of faith the New Baptists shared with the Mennonites. They abhorred war and violence. They had lived with it, suffered from it, and knew its tragedy. To them, war was incompatible with the Christian concept of love exemplified by Jesus. Force was contrary to the clear teachings of the New Testament. Some of them may have witnessed and felt the effects of force in religion. Not wanting to repeat the same errors, they were very careful not to force their religion upon others, even their own children. To them, religion must be the free, uncoerced response of the individual to God as revealed by Christ. There is no known record of anyone during the first generation being baptized younger than seventeen.

Because of the New Baptists' strong emphasis on trine immersion and their tendency toward exclusivism in a tightly knit community, the question of "universal restoration" of the soul to God was repeatedly raised. Mack believed that all those persons who die outside of salvation in Christ would be punished in the torment of hell, "but that the torture should continue entirely without end is not sustained by the scriptures."[34]

Mack truly believed that the way of divine love would eventually triumph and that all people would one day find their way back to God. He believed that God would still extend an opportunity to all for purification after death, even though he felt that those "restored" after death would never achieve the high state of bliss possible for those who chose to follow Christ in this life.

Mack was reluctant to proclaim publicly the doctrine of universal restoration, fearing that people would be encouraged to postpone their ultimate decision until after death, thus losing the benefits of life in Christian community.

In all of his preaching, guidance, and shepherding, Mack had two major goals: (1) "that all who call themselves Christian should live as children of one household"[35] and (2) that all believers should avoid "the great abuses which have prevailed among all Christian parties."[36] With these goals in mind, Mack directed his energy toward creating in the Schwarzenau congregation a new style of life, and toward spreading their unique understanding of the faith quietly to others who were searching for a different and more satisfying way.

CHAPTER VIII

Years of Evangelism
1709-1712

The Schwarzenau congregation grew rapidly, becoming a strong, cohesive group. In some rather remarkable fashion, Mack had led the New Baptists through their earliest controversies and had helped them establish a stable style of life which included within its structure the opportunity for continuing growth and renewal. It was a simple, communal fellowship.

Though still in his early thirties, Mack exhibited surprising emotional maturity. Not gifted with oratorical flair or dramatic charisma, as Hochman was, Mack was blessed with other skills. He possessed great patience, perseverance, and ingenious organizational gifts. For a stagecoach ride from Hamburg to Frankfurt, Hochman would have been a tremendously interesting traveling companion; but for practical small business management, Mack would have had far better potential. Hochmann was a visionary, a dreamer of dreams, an incomparable enthusiast. Mack was a man who turned dreams into action—a man of credibility, sincerity, and genuine religious devotion.

Mack had been especially successful in helping to develop within the New Baptist community a strong sense of identity and mutuality. For displaced persons trying to find refuge in strange places, a strong sense of communal identity met a very real need. It was, without doubt, this emphasis on community which helped to attract other Pietists to the New Baptist gatherings.

Evangelistic in their expression of faith, and enthusiastic about the religious freedom they enjoyed, the New Baptists were exceptionally persuasive in their presentation of baptism by immersion as an essential factor in faith-commitment, and in their conviction that some kind of disciplined community was essential in order to fulfill New Testament commands.

By 1715 the congregation had grown so much that Alexander Mack, Jr., later described it as a "large congregation." By 1720, twelve years after the first eight baptisms had been performed, there were approximately two hundred members. A folk-tradition told in Schwarzenau today refers to a lot located near the Eder River where the early Brethren supposedly met after outgrowing the capacity of their homes to hold meetings. This lot is still called the "*Täufergarten*" (Baptist Garden).[1]

In the first year of the congregation's existence, many baptisms took place, one of which involved a seventy-year-old man who almost drowned in the process. Most baptismal services, however, were uneventful and were discreetly performed, for the Baptists were not eager to antagonize their neighbors needlessly. Although strong in his own convictions, Mack was not insensitive to the rights and the feelings of others.

Most of the Baptists lived in small houses or huts in the hills above Schwarzenau. Many new converts settled in an area called the "Valley of the Huts." Others lived in villages close by. Many were very poor and were literally fed and clothed through the sharing of possessions by those who had plenty. Mack was especially generous, but a fairly large group contributed to the common need. George Grebe, Luke Vetter, Michael Eckerlin, Jacob Bossert, and Andrew Boni were all men of means and respected property owners.

Success frequently breeds enmity, and the Schwarzenau Brethren were not spared. As their congregation flourished, criticism from Separatists increased. Although Hochmann likely attended the New Baptists' services for a short time after his return to Schwarzenau from Nürnberg, he was so opposed to their "cultish forms" of baptism and feetwashing that he soon stopped. Not "individualistic" in seeking a solitary relationship with God, Hochmann simply felt that he could maintain a deep spiritual fellowship with other Christians without baptism, formal church structures, hierarchies of authority, or scheduled programs and meetings. Hochmann wanted to be free to follow, at any moment, the guidance of the Spirit. "The local *Taufer's* strict law and human yoke," he declared, "are completely intolerable to a spirit made free by the blood of Christ."[2]

Understandably, Hochmann's attitude and criticism were sorely felt by these New Baptists who had considered him their primary spiritual leader. Mack, who had loved Hochmann as a friend, worked with him as a brother, and followed him as a disciple, must have been the most disappointed of all. Tension between the two grew and is recorded in a story told about an Anabaptist gathering held somewhere in Switzerland.

Mack was the principal speaker for this occasion, but Hochmann also had been invited to speak. Hochmann's message was so upsetting to Mack that he "openly condemned him before all the people. He called him a hypocrite, a false prophet, and other things."

Hochmann did not openly reply to Mack's criticism during the meeting but, following the closing prayer, he stood up, walked over to Mack and embraced him with the "holy kiss." Then in a tender fashion, he said: "Dear Brother Mack, when you are in heaven and see me arrive there also, then you will rejoice and say, 'Oh, look. There comes also our dear Hochmann.' "[3]

A few months after the baptism, in January 1709, a definite and complete break brought an end to the relationship between Mack and Hochmann. Except for chance encounters at Pietistic meetings, they apparently had no further affiliation, though they continued to live not far distant from each other in Schwarzenau from 1709 to 1720. In 1709 Hochman built himself a "little haven of peace" which he called *Friedensburg* and in which he lived until his death in 1721.

As time passed, Hochman became increasingly vocal in his criticism of the Baptist position. In 1714 he remarked in a letter that he had learned through bitter experience that many of those who had idealistically left their established churches had then proceeded to erect a new "sectarian Babylon and so barricaded themselves with it."[4] Hochmann eventually opposed the Baptist movement openly and publicly, reiterating that he did not need the "outward dipping as the good Alexander Mack believes."[5]

Although rumors later circulated in America that Hochmann had eventually been baptized by Mack, there is no such proof, and a great deal of evidence would indicate that Mack and Hochmann were never reconciled. Although Mack was deeply disturbed and hurt by this situation, he did not allow himself to brood upon it to the detriment of his responsibilities.

A more seriously disturbing situation claimed Mack's attention. In the spring of 1709, disquieting news reached Mack concerning his old friend, Martin Lucas, in Heidelberg. A group of Pietists meeting in Lucas's home had been arrested for violating the law prohibiting religious gatherings in private homes. An inquisitional hearing was held. Lucas admitted that he had not attended church in four years, feeling that a house built by men's hands for the worship of God was unnecessary. He believed that the established churches were so sinful in their structure and practice that they no longer had the "grace of God." One of his inquisitors asked Lucas, "What exactly is a Pietist?"

Lucas replied that a Pietist is "a devout Christian who leads a pious life in Christ and God."[6]

Another official asked Lucas whether he knew any person who had the "grace of explaining the scriptures as did the Apostles." Lucas responded without hesitation: "Alexander Mack, who is now at Schwarzenau in Wittgenstein, and many in the Marienborn area, even a nobleman, by name of Ernst Hochmann."[7]

When he was asked to describe a Pietistic gathering, he said:

> When they come together they sing two or three hymns, as God moves them; then they open the Bible and whatever they find they read and explain it according to the understanding given to them by God, for the edification of their brethren. After they have read, they fall to their knees, raise their hands to God and pray for the authorities, that God might move them to punish the evil and protect the good; then they praise God that He has created them for this purpose.[8]

Lucas explained that the Pietists had no set time for their meetings, but were ready to "come together on Sundays, holidays, or workdays as God moves them."[9] He pointed out that the Pietists had a community of loving responsibility to one another. As long as anyone was in need, the others shared from their own portion of abundance.

Following this interrogation, Lucas and three others were ordered to join one of the established state churches. Since Lucas and his wife could not "in good conscience" obey this order, they were banished to a province in southern Holland and not allowed to take their children with them. This was an unusually harsh punishment, one of the most cruel in Pietistic history. The Lucas home was confiscated and sold to pay two guardians for the care of the Lucas children. There is no record to indicate that Martin Lucas and his wife ever saw their children again.

Several years of exile passed before Martin Lucas and his wife were able to leave Holland. Not permitted to return to the Palatinate, they settled in Düdelsheim in the Marienborn territory. Here they were warmly accepted by the New Baptists, who helped them become reestablished.

Mack had not been surprised by the order of exile Lucas had received, but he had been horrified by the vindictive separation of parents and children. He was gravely concerned for his friend who had suffered much for his faith: imprisonment twice in Heidelberg, once in Schriesheim, once in Mannheim, and now exile and the seizure of his children. It seemed too much for Lucas and his wife to bear. Mack feared that conditions in some areas were becoming even more oppressive.

By contrast, Wittgenstein continued to be a haven of religious freedom under Count Henry. His brother-in-law, however, Count Charles Louis of Sayn-Wittgenstein-Sayn, was far less willing to permit actions which he did not personally approve. On July 1, 1709, he wrote to Count Henry, protesting his tolerance of that "fanatic pack at Schwarzenau" and recommending that they be exterminated by "banishment from the empire with fire and sword."[10]

On August 20, 1709, Count Henry replied to his brother-in-law, defending his policy of religious freedom by appealing to reason, natural decency, the teachings of Jesus, and the principles of the Protestant church. "No one will convince me," he wrote, "that it is my responsibility and office as a ruler to prosecute with pope-ish reprimand" those who allegedly err in their religious ideas.

This reply infuriated Charles Louis. Within a week, he answered with a fiery message, charging Henry with violation of imperial law and the destruction of his land by these miserably poor refugees. He called the New Baptists "rabble-like family defamers" leading a "fanatical movement."[11]

By 1710, Count Charles Louis had produced a detailed list of charges against the Baptists. This document became known as "Enclosure Q" and was sent to various political leaders in an attempt to pressure Henry to change his policies. Enclosure Q specified the following charges (paraphrased):

1. They organize private meetings where males and females are permitted to teach whatever the Spirit moves them.
2. They deny their own infant baptism, refuse to baptize their children, and engage in notorious re-baptism.
3. Rather than going to church for the sacrament of communion, they engage in the *Agape* (love feast) in their secret meetings.
4. They discard considerations of social rank, honors, positions, respect for parents, respect of wives for husbands, obedience to authorities. They also reject oaths, courts, and court proceedings.[12]

Charles Louis' efforts were not entirely in vain. The ruler of Hesse, Count Henry's uncle, was so concerned that on November 25, 1710, he wrote to Count Henry chastizing him for tolerating "enthusiasts, fanatics, and godless sectarians" in his territory. He urged Henry to expel this "most scandalous pack" immediately.

Count Henry replied again in defense of religious freedom and particularly in defense of the New Baptist sect, a people "who have led quiet lives to this date."[13] He was pleased by the responsible, law-abiding citizenship of the Baptist Brethren. They paid their taxes regularly, obeyed the civil laws created to guarantee order in the affairs of the village, and broke only those laws which conflicted with their primary loyalty to God.

Although Alexander Mack may not have known about this correspondence, he was certainly aware that Count Henry had taken an unpopular position in the empire and had to resist many pressures from other rulers against his policies. Like Count Henry, most of the citizens and Separatists of Schwarzenau were tolerant of the New Baptists. One such Separatist was a Swiss nobleman, Nicholas Samuel de Treytorrens, who had also known persecution, in his homeland, for his beliefs. Giving all of his property to the poor, he went into voluntary exile, settling in Schwarzenau in 1709, and living simply, in the manner of the Baptists. Although there is no evidence that he joined their congregation, he was definitely an admiring friend and neighbor.

Some of the Separatists, however, were very unsympathetic, continuing to cast aspersions against the New Baptists. One such was Christopher Seebach, a noted Lutheran minister who had been removed from his parish and who had established himself in Schwarzenau. Seebach published a treatise against "water baptism," which, he said, leads to a "dreadful sectarianism."[14] Although Seebach was unalterably opposed to water baptism, he was even more opposed to coercion of conscience. In one tract he denounced the use of soldiers to baptize with force those infants whose parents denied them this rite. "Never did John the Baptist, or a disciple of Jesus, baptize anyone by force,"[15] he wrote.

Although Charles Louis in Enclosure Q had criticized "the miller in Schwarzenau" who had "not let his children be baptized,"[16] it is quite doubtful that any of his own children had ever been forcibly baptized. Count Henry would not have permitted it. Seebach's statement, though, illustrates the intolerant spirit of the times and the shaky foundation upon which the New Baptists and the Mennonites' freedom of religious conscience rested.

In 1711, Mack was invited by several Baptist families in the Marienborn area to visit their community for evangelistic work and to baptize any converts. Mack was welcomed into the home of the Jacob Bossert family of Himbach, not far from Büdingen, where the castle and the court of the local count were located. Mack knew that this count was opposed to public religious ceremonies and to the formation of new religious organizations. And he knew also that the task he was prepared to do was illegal and endangered his freedom. He chose to accept the invitation, not in defiant rebellion but in humble submission to what he believed was an even higher law.

Among the people who welcomed him to this community was the Martin Lucas family. Mack's empathy for their grief at the loss of their children when they had been exiled to Holland made him especially happy to see these dear friends again. Daniel Ritter and his wife, who eventually migrated to Krefeld, were also members of this group.

There are no records to indicate how the Ritters, the Bosserts, or the Lucases had been baptized, but it is quite likely that they had either lived in Schwarzenau for a time or had traveled there just for a baptismal occasion.

As was his custom, Mack spoke to his friends about his vision of Christian community built upon discipleship and love for both God and neighbor. After such sermons, he always included his statement of faith that adult baptism by immersion was the New Testament symbol of Christian commitment and entrance into a new life. At this meeting, a young woman, daughter of the widow Eva Elizabeth Hoffman (who had previously been baptized by Mack), responded to his appeal and requested baptism.

Mack realized the possible consequences, but his commitment to this new way of life was stronger than his fear. On August 21, 1711, Mack and his friends accompanied *Frau* Hoffman and her two daughters to the winding Seame Brook flowing through the woods near Düdelsheim for the baptism. Gathering beneath an old oak tree, they knelt reverently with hands uplifted for prayer. At the close of the prayer, Mack entered the stream with a long stick to measure the depth of the water. Finding a suitable place, he invited the applicant into the water. Perhaps fear of the water or fear of the consequences made her reluctant to enter the stream. But, encouraged by her mother and the others, she waded into the cold water and knelt before Mack to receive the rite.

"Are you willing to renounce the world, and the devil, and your own flesh?" Mack asked.

"Yes."

"Thereupon," Mack continued, placing his hands gently upon her braided hair and immersing her in the flowing water, "I baptize you in the name of the Father, and of the Son, and of the Holy Spirit." A prayer of dedication followed.

As the two waded out of the water, Mack said to her softly, "Now your spirit and faith are strengthened."[17] The young woman then joined several women who were holding up a sheet behind a tree, so that she could change into dry clothes. As she dressed, the group sang one of their familiar hymns:

> Lord Jesus Christ, turn toward us;
> send to us thy Holy Spirit;
> Rule us with grace and charity
> And lead us on the road to truth.

> Open our mouths to sing thy praise,
> Prepare our hearts for pure devotion,
> Increase our faith; strengthen our understanding
> That thy name will become well known to us.

> Until we sing with the hosts of God,
> Holy, Holy, is God the Lord.
> Then we'll look upon thee face to face,
> In eternal joy and holy light.

> Honor be to the Father and to the Son
> And to the Holy Spirit all enthroned;
> The Holy Trinity
> Be praised and honored for all eternity.[18]

When the service was completed, the men greeted each other with the "holy kiss." Likewise, the women performed the same ritual among themselves. Then together, they walked with quiet joy to the Martin Lucas home for a concluding devotional service. All of them were aware of the possible consequences of the day's events.

At least five witnesses, and perhaps many more, had observed the baptism. Count Charles August was greatly disturbed. On August 31, his councilors wrote to the local pastor and to the count's deputy administrator for a complete report. The next day this report was sent. It was straightforward and factual with no suggestion of judgment.

The court councilors were not as tolerant. They did not want such activity and controversy to begin in their territory. On September 4, they summoned *Frau* Hoffman and her daughter to appear before the council. After hearing the case, the count's protection was withdrawn from the widow and she was ordered to leave the Marienborn area. Alexander Mack was also ordered to leave, and a final statement was sent to all the villagers: "No one is to shelter him under penalty of arbitrary punishment."[19]

Frau Hoffman told her friends of the council's decision. Feeling that it was quite unfair, they asked Mack to intercede on her behalf. On September 5, 1711, Mack composed a respectful and reasonable appeal, hoping to persuade the count of the unfairness of this judgment. Mack argued that she had not baptized or been baptized in the count's territory. Yet she had been examined and punished, even though the council had not found her guilty of any violation of the law.

In his fervor, Mack tried to convince Count Charles August that immersion of adults was the only truly biblical baptism. In closing, Mack wrote that he would be happy to be instructed, if "learned theologians" could prove him in error. This letter of Mack's is the only one of his letters, apparently, that has survived to the present day.[20] It did not succeed in its intention. The count was adamant. *Frau* Hoffman must leave the territory.

Mack did not understand that his ban from Marienborn was permanent. Several weeks later he returned to Düdelsheim to conduct another baptismal service, this time on October 13, 1711. At this service Esbert Bender of Dillenberg, Augustus Pfeil from near Kassel, the widow Geyer, and an unnamed woman living with Widow Hoffman at Himbach were baptized. There were six witnesses: the Lucases, the Ritters, Widow Hoffman, and her daughter.

These four fledgling members were immediately called before the count's representative in Düdelsheim. Since the policy of these New Baptists was to be open and honest, fearless in their allegiance to God, the new converts confirmed the fact of their baptism. A report was sent to the council at Büdingen. On October 15, the council sent the following orders to Düdelsheim (paraphrased):

1. No more baptisms are to be permitted.
2. Mack must leave the area within twenty-four hours, or he will be physically expelled.
3. All the baptized and those who were present must vacate the territory within eight days.
4. The count's representative must personally see to it that these orders are carried out.[21]

To emphasize the seriousness of the edict, a directive to the count's representative at Himbach ordered him to rid the territory of Widow Hoffman within twenty-four hours.

Presumably this order was carried out, for a list of the Brethren in that area, published in 1714, contained neither her name nor those of her daughters. There is no further record of her involvement with New Baptists in any area.

Mack returned to Schwarzenau for the birth of his third child, Alexander Mack, Jr., whom he did not have baptized at the village church. All the others who participated with Mack in the October 13 baptismal service also left Marienborn or returned to the established church, with the exception of Daniel Ritter and his wife, who somehow found a way to remain. Martin Lucas and his wife fled with their children[22] to the city of Krefeld on the lower Rhine River. In extreme poverty, they were forced to accept public welfare. Esbert Bender, a wool spinner, and his wife followed Mack to Schwarzenau and later to Pennsylvania. Jacob Bossert and his wife, both Palatinate and Marienborn refugees, also fled to Schwarzenau and later to America.

The New Baptists were not especially discouraged by these events. Perhaps they became a bit more discreet, but there was no more harassment for about a year. Since Count Charles August refused to allow baptisms in Marienborn, new converts in that area had to go to Schwarzenau for baptism.

Marie Elizabeth Diehl, becoming convinced that immersion was a necessary rite, requested her husband John's permission to travel to Schwarzenau for baptism. He refused to allow it. When Mack heard of this problem, he felt that he must, as the Baptists' spiritual leader, return to Düdelsheim once again. He arrived for this third baptismal event in Marienborn on November 4, 1712. When J. L. Winter, the count's representative, learned of Mack's arrival, he promptly sent him a warning and an order to perform no baptisms. Mack sent back a message that he was spending the night with good friends and would be leaving in the morning. Because the usual time for baptisms had been in the early morning, the authorities may have planned to patrol the area by the Seame Brook the following morning. In anticipation of such a possibility, Mack apparently decided to hold the service in the late evening. Marie Elizabeth Diehl, the wife of John Naas, and two unknown persons were immersed in the Seame Brook into a new life in Jesus Christ.

When J. L. Winter received this news early the next morning, he was furious. He ordered Mack to go straight to the village inn and remain there until he received further instructions. Then he summoned *Frau* Diehl to his home and accused her of breaking the law. *Frau* Diehl replied simply that she must obey God rather than the authorities. Unable to argue against that apostolic statement, Winter let her go.

Mack was promptly expelled from the area and forbidden ever to return. This order was sealed by the shaking of hands, which to the New Baptists was as binding as taking an oath. So far as is known, Mack never violated this agreement.

All the newly baptized converts were then ordered to appear before the Marienborn presbytery for examination and appropriate action. In all of Europe, the accused could scarcely have been more fortunate. One of the panel was Samuel König, a noted Pietist and former companion of Hochmann. A former resident of Schwarzenau, König had returned to the Reformed Church, becoming a pastor at Büdingen in 1710. König had no desire to sit in judgment upon these Baptists. He asked to be excused from the hearing, but the count refused, writing to König to emphasize his own intention to govern benevolently but insisting that measures must be taken to quiet and correct the "spoiled cravings of the spirit which always desire something new."[23] Other members of the consistory, in varying degrees, were also rather sympathetic to the Baptist-Brethren.

On December 1, 1712, the investigation was made and the converts were admonished not "to lay too much emphasis on baptism, but on the contrary, to show all others most brotherly friendship."[24] The consistory then composed a report for the count, in which they recommended that the religious protection of the state not be revoked. They pointed out that Baptists were now tolerated in other areas and that immersion was no longer a novelty.

The problem of ministerial leadership in the Marienborn area demanded immediate attention. With Mack unable to return, the church there needed a minister empowered to baptize. John Naas was anointed as this leader. The number of converts steadily increased so that by 1714 Naas had a congregation of approximately fifty members.

It was a rather tempestuous period. There was little prospect that the authorities would extend protection and tolerance to these people. Their security was shaky, and, in addition, a very aggressive congregation of the Community of True Inspiration had been established in Himbach. It was a Pietistic, mystical movement led by Eberhard Gruber and John Frederick Rock. Its presence increased the political-religious tension which already existed.

Mack's efforts had reaped a small harvest but had stirred up a storm, creating a crisis which would eventually lead to the exile of all Baptists from the Marienborn area.

CHAPTER IX

YEARS OF OPPOSITION
1713-1715

Opposition to the New Baptist sect was growing throughout the land. The winds of change were stirring as governments and religious groups actively opposed them.

Eberhard Louis Gruber, a noteworthy Pietist who had migrated to the Marienborn area in 1707, became one of Mack's most formidable antagonists. Bringing with him a zealous commitment to a nonconforming approach in religion, an incisive mind, and a mystical spirit, he, too, was searching for a more satisfying expression of faith.

In 1713, Gruber visited Schwarzenau and became well acquainted with the rapidly growing Baptists. There he and Mack participated in a public debate concerning matters of faith and practice. Gruber submitted to Mack a series of questions concerning the immersion of adults, the establishment of a new sect, and the relationship of the New Baptists to other Christians. This dialog was published at Schwarzenau in July 1713 under the title *Basic Questions,*[1] the first publication of the Brethren. Although it has been reprinted numerous times, none of the original copies have survived.

Gruber's questions were penetrating but never hostile. Basically, Gruber attacked the narrowness of the Baptist claim that only those Christians who had been immersed were of the true church of Christ. Mack insisted that a remnant of the church had practiced immersion ever since the time of Christ. Gruber was just as insistent that, for a long period of church history, adult immersion was not practiced at all. Mack, however, was not able to provide convincing proof for his position.

When Gruber questioned Mack about the "undeniable witnesses

of truth" in Christendom who had not been immersed, Mack replied that he was willing to leave their judgment to God. "You will know them by their fruits," Mack said, defining fruits as a "willingness to walk in the teachings of Jesus"[2]—and therefore a willingness to be immersed! Gruber was not convinced.

"Is water baptism so absolutely necessary that positively no one can be saved without it . . . ?"[3] he asked.

Mack replied that salvation was not found through the baptism, but through faith in the Lord Jesus Christ. Therefore, he continued, "a believer who desires to be baptized but cannot obtain it . . . is still saved."[4]

Gruber pushed him further. The situations where flowing water would not be available for immersion would be extremely rare. "Were then," he asked, "all those who lived and died after the time of the early Christians, who did not receive baptism in the original form, completely lost and damned . . . ?"[5]

Mack replied simply: "If they had . . . true faith in Jesus . . . they were certainly saved . . . even if they had not obtained outward baptism."[6] This dialog thus forced Mack to modify his earlier position on immersion.

Gruber then questioned Mack from another perspective. If the Baptists were not setting up immersion as an absolute precondition for salvation, were they not introducing a "New Papacy" and attempting to reintroduce "salvation through works"?

Mack answered that true faith issued from obedience to Christ, who clearly taught that immersion was a sign of new birth. "No salvation," he continued, "is promised for a single work done without faith."[7] Mack clearly repudiated any idea that baptism *per se* has intrinsic efficacy.

Gruber asked if the Baptists felt they had a direct calling from God to institute their form of baptism. Mack replied that they did feel they had such a calling but that it was not accompanied by signs or miracles. Each individual must decide for himself whether the Baptist view of baptism is truly from God.[8]

Other questions were raised by Gruber concerning the age when children could be accepted for baptism, the use of the ban against wayward members, and the relationship of the Baptists to those Christians who chose not to be immersed.

Mack's responses were simple. Children who were able to "prove and profess" their faith were old enough for baptism. The ban was to be used against wayward Christians in order to move them to repentance and renewed strength in the Lord. Only those Christians who had been willing to submit themselves to immersion as an act of faith-obedience could be rightfully accepted as brothers and sisters within their Christian community.

Gruber raised a more poignant question concerning the relationship of the New Baptists to the Pietists, such as Hochmann, with whom they had once been closely related.

Mack, without bitterness, replied that the Pietists live by their own principles. He expressed their attitude in almost contemporary terms: "Leave me alone in my own will, opinion, and action, and I will leave you alone in yours; we will love each other and be brethren."[9] Mack called this eighteenth-century version of "doing your own thing" a "ruinous, hypocritical love." He emphatically repudiated this principle, for Christian love, he believed, is in no way an unconcerned love, but is "the kind of love which hates and reproves wickedness and evil."[10]

Mack's understanding of Christian commitment was strongly social, implying that an individualistic ethic would not be capable of dealing with corporate evil, whether in business, religion, or politics. Christian love, according to Mack, led Jesus to protest corruption in the temple and to die on a cross. A Christian cannot retreat into a haven of solitary peace and self-satisfaction. Christians are called to a new life in Christ Jesus. Out of his own experience as a child, fleeing from armies, sharing food with others in hiding, caring for one another's needs when homes were pillaged and burned, Mack had strong feelings about the importance of a caring community.

In his final question, Gruber accused Mack of seeking to establish a new church. Mack vehemently denied this charge. "We indeed have neither a new church nor any new laws. We only want to remain in simplicity and true faith in the original church which Jesus founded through his blood."[11]

When the debate ended, Gruber was not convinced, for Mack's assertions were less than adequately supported. Some of his conclusions had questionable merit. Yet he showed an admirable spirit of searching, a willingness to modify his positions, and a wholehearted dedication to the elusive truth that sets persons free.

Both Mack and Gruber made an honest effort to be respectful to each other, reconciling, and affirmative. Neither demonstrated the kind of rancor and bitterness which characterized much eighteenth century religious debate.

Broken relationships leave their scars, and Mack's dogmatic responses to Gruber may well have been a partially defensive reaction to the criticism leveled against him by Hochmann. In the year that *Basic Questions* was published, Hochmann wrote his last will and testament. In it he bequeathed his home to two close friends, Christian Erb and Matthew Lemser. No mention was made of Mack or any other person who had become a Baptist. It seems quite possible that some of Mack's rigidity and legalism during this period could have been a reaction to the disapproving presence of Hochmann within the village.

In 1714, Anna Margaret Mack, who had been a great source of strength to the Mack family in its flight from Schriesheim and its establishment of a new home in Wittgenstein, received the sad news that her father, John Valentine Kling, had died. She had been very close to her father, and both had suffered for their Pietistic faith. In the same year, she gave birth to her fourth child, Christina, a frail infant who lived for only six years.

In spite of the many extended absences of her husband, Anna Margaret had been able to maintain a stable family life. She was not a leader in the Baptist movement, but her quiet endurance and strength often provided encouragement to others during recurring periods of difficulty.

By 1714 the Baptist movement in Wittgenstein reached its peak in growth and was leveling off. In contrast, the Marienborn area was experiencing a surge of growth. Two new leaders had migrated from Eppstein to Marienborn: Christian Liebe and Abraham Dubois. Brumbaugh described Liebe as an "eloquent, gifted evangelist."[12] During 1714, Liebe visited numerous Pietistic meetings in the Rhine valley, eventually traveling as far as Switzerland, where he courageously baptized a number of new converts. When he arrived in the city of Berne, he was arrested for spreading Anabaptist beliefs. On June 6, 1714, he and four ministers of the Swiss Brethren (Mennonites) were condemned to life imprisonment as galley slaves under the jurisdiction of the king of Sicily.

This news was shocking! It was the harshest sentence any of the Baptists had ever been given. With sadness and a kind of holy resignation, little clusters of Liebe's brothers and sisters received this news in both Marienborn and Schwarzenau. In their beleaguered condition, they felt politically impotent; but, in their faith, they believed that God's justice would ultimately prevail.

Following their sentencing, these prisoners were detained in a Bernese dungeon for several weeks, then forced to walk, chained hand and foot across the high, snow-covered Alps to Turin, Italy. Here, they were thrown in another dungeon. Working at hard labor under unbelievably squalid conditions, these prisoners deteriorated so rapidly that one of the Swiss Brethren soon died.

The Schwarzenau congregation wanted to extend some kind of support and expression of love to the imprisoned Liebe. Perhaps because of the recent birth of his fourth child, Mack felt he could not leave. Andrew Boni was commissioned to travel to Turin with supplies and money for Liebe.

In the spring, after spending a winter of indescribable squalor in the Turin dungeon, Liebe and the others were sent to Palermo to be placed on a Sicilian ship. There a second Swiss brother died. Isolated from their friends and relatives, enduring backbreaking work under the Mediterranean sun, and confined to the cramped quarters of a galley ship, these prisoners were probably unaware of the extensive efforts being made for their release by both Mennonites and Baptists in Holland and Germany.

Finally, the Swiss nobleman, Nicholas Samuel de Treytorrens, who had settled in Schwarzenau, volunteered his services. Believing that his knowledge of the situation in Berne might be helpful, he made plans for his journey. A letter from Liebe's mother and other pertinent documentation were secured, along with a large sum of money donated probably by Mack for expenses. Nicholas traveled to Berne, where he was promptly arrested and sentenced to banishment. However, in the hectic days before he left the city, Nicholas, surprisingly, was able to procure letters of release from the proper authorities for Liebe and the two surviving Swiss Brethren. This release was based upon the condition that none of the four ever set foot in Berne again without the expressed permission of the Bernese government or by some miraculous act of God.

After spending more than two years as prisoners, under the harshest conditions, Liebe and the two Mennonites welcomed their benefactor with unrestrained gratitude. It was now the spring of 1716. Carefully avoiding the Canton of Berne, Nicholas and Liebe journeyed north to Eppstein, where Liebe visited his aging mother and learned that the Baptists had been banished from the Marienborn area.

While Liebe was gone, several events had precipitated the eviction of the Baptists. In May 1715, John Naas baptized Gottfried Neumann, Peter Becker, and Becker's wife in the presence of a rather large group of spectators. The state councilors were infuriated at such a blatantly disrespectful act. Despite its illegality, and despite their repeated warnings, the Baptists had once again performed some public baptisms. What made the matter even more serious was that two of those baptized were highly respected citizens of Düdelsheim, and not insignificant refugees.

Naas was ordered to leave the area in forty-eight hours, and those present at the baptism within eight days—never to return. The situation changed somewhat when Gottfried Neumann appeared before the council. A former Lutheran theologian, and the most highly educated convert to the New Baptist movement, Neumann was a very persuasive person. He convinced the council that an eight-day limit would cause undue hardship. They extended the limit, and Neumann did not leave until a year later.

During that time, Neumann became quite irritated by the "pharisaical sectarian spirit" of the New Baptists and began to persuade people to refuse baptism. For a period of time he became actively associated with the Inspirationists. Later he became a Moravian, and is widely recognized as one of their greatest hymn writers. In spite of his break with the New Baptists, Neumann conceded in a letter to Francke in 1719 that the Brethren were "single-minded and good souls." "They displayed . . . ," he added, "a great earnestness and zeal in their behavior and conduct through which many were moved and drawn into their circle."[13]

This congregation of the Community of True Inspiration at Himbach was as illegal as the New Baptist movement. The Inspirationists, who believed that they were acting according to direct guidance from God, vigorously proclaimed their faith and boldly denounced wickedness in high places. No official of the early eighteenth century was inclined to ignore such attacks. Reacting with anger, by the summer of 1715 the authorities had succeeded in eliminating both the New Baptists and the Inspirationists from the Marienborn area.

Most of the Marienborn Baptists, including John Naas and Peter Becker, settled in Krefeld near the Dutch border. Here they were cordially welcomed by the Mennonites, who were strong in that area. When Liebe returned from his imprisonment, he also joined the Baptist community in Krefeld. Understandably, Naas was reluctant to relinquish his leadership to Liebe, and some tension developed between them.

A few of the members from Marienborn settled in Schwarzenau, readily accepting Mack's leadership there. Unfortunately for Mack, Gruber and his Inspirationists also chose to settle in Schwarzenau. In June of 1715, Gruber organized a congregation in direct competition with the New Baptists for the allegiance of the Separatists in the vicinity.

Under increasing pressure from the Inspirationists, Mack wrote another tract. He hoped it would be more effective than *Basic Questions* had been in adequately and persuasively defending New Baptist positions. Mack published this tract in 1715, calling it *Rights and Ordinances of the House of God*. It concerned the "rights" which the true church of Christ demands of the Christians and the ordinances, or laws, which regulate their behavior in the Christian community (*Gemeinde*). This tract was divided into nineteen sections, each one concerning a specific issue. As would be expected, baptism was the first issue considered.

Mack used a dialog between father and son as his format, which turned out to be more stilted than that of *Basic Questions*. His arrangement was based on the Dordrecht Confession of 1632, printed in the *Martyrs' Mirror* by the Mennonites.

To introduce the first section, on baptism, Mack begins with the son complaining to his father that he had been teased by people who practice infant baptism. The father responds with much the same arguments as those Mack had given in *Basic Questions*.

Mack's second section concerns the Lord's Supper. He insists that nonmenbers and "obvious sinners"[14] may not partake of the Lord's Supper, in which there should always be an atmosphere of love and mutuality.

His third section deals with excommunication. Mack takes the position of Menno Simons, the outstanding Mennonite leader of the sixteenth century, that the ban and excommunication are necessary disciplines used to protect the purity of the church.

Fourth, he considers the taking of oaths. Most Anabaptists of his time maintained that a simple "yes" or "no" was sufficient, since the Christian was a person of truth.

In his fifth section, on worship, Mack clearly rejects the mystical and individualistic views of "high talking people" like Gruber and

Rock. Worship is for the interpretation of the scriptures and for the glory of God. Mack believed there is an "internal word," a kind of inner conscience which guides the Christian who totally commits his life to the Lord Jesus Christ, and which is revealed through private devotions and corporate worship as the "external word" (the Bible) is studied.

In his section on the punishment of unbelievers, the son asks the father about human destiny. Then he asks whether the torture of the damned will last "forever without end."[15] The father replies that the belief that the torture will continue forever "is not sustained by the scriptures."[16] The son shows interest in the idea of ultimate restoration of all persons to fellowship with God, and the father responds that, although the unsaved at death will ultimately be restored, they will never be as happily blessed as those who choose Christ freely in this life.

In his final section, Mack chooses the title, "Fatherly Advice." This illustrates clearly the way he understood his role as minister and spiritual leader. "You will not find any other holiness in the Old and New Testament than in doing the will of God. This has always been, and it will ever be the salvation of the soul."[17]

Mack was as much a child of his age as Luther or Calvin was of theirs, his faith having been shaped by Mennonite and Pietistic thought. In spite of his deep desire to remain open to new light from the scriptures, when a faith experience proved meaningful to him, it was difficult not to make it into an ordinance, imposing it as a norm on others.

Looking at Mack's tract from a literary point of view, *Rights and Ordinances* is repetitious, tedious, and lacking in style. From a theological perspective, it tends to be legalistic, so much so that it makes one wonder whether Mack ever really understood what Paul said in Romans and Galatians about law and grace. To make one's relationship to God conditioned upon a particular mode of baptism reveals a sad constriction of vision. It is quite fair to say that in trying to correct the error of infant baptism Mack went to the other extreme. The life that he lived was far better than his writings. Mack did not write in order to produce a literary masterpiece or even a theological treatise. He wrote primarily to challenge other Separatists to reconsider and reevaluate their attitudes toward baptism, Christian community, and style of living.

A careful examination of Mack's writing shows that in 1715 his four major faith assumptions were as follows:

1. Acceptance of the historic doctrines of Christianity.

Mack was not interested in theological controversy. Of what importance to life was a debate over the nature of God? He accepted without question the basic teachings of historic Christianity: monotheism, the divine nature and the true humanity of Jesus, Christ's sacrificial death and resurrection, the reality of heaven and hell, and the need of human beings for salvation from sin.

2. Acceptance of the New Testament as the Christian's only creed.

To Mack, creeds were composed by men, but the Bible had been inspired by God, with final authority resting in the New Testament. Suspicious of creeds which he felt had contributed to the divisiveness and the tragedy of his childhood years in Schriesheim, Mack rejected them all, even though he believed in many of the ideas they expressed. The early Brethren were sometimes accused of worshiping the New Testament because they accepted this principle so nearly completely.

3. Acceptance of no force in religion.

Mack viewed the overriding of the individual conscience as wrong. Therefore, baptism had to follow the freely made choice of each individual. Mack further assumed that participation in war, or in any coercive institution, such as government, was incompatible with the spirit and the teachings of the New Testament.

4. Acceptance of new visions of truth.

Mack recognized that he was indebted to the scholarship of his day. The works of the Pietist, Gottfried Arnold, had greatly influenced him in his youth. The thought and the warmth of Hochmann and other Pietistic leaders had been an important influence in his development. The discipline and the dedication of the Mennonites had impressed him. His own personal experiences and observations had partially determined the direction of his faith. He accepted all of these, and readily admitted that some of his ideas had been modified and changed over the years. He recognized that the future could reveal new truth, and he wanted to be open to hear that truth. But, for the present, he must be loyal to the truth as it was currently revealed to him. It was at this point that he tended toward dogmatic exclusivism. Yet, an important principle of his faith was that the Christian life is one of growth and change.

On the basis of these four assumptions, Mack vigorously defended in *Rights and Ordinances* five marks of Christian commitment:

1. Faith-obedience.

Mack maintained that salvation is obtained through loving faith-obedience to the spirit and the teachings of Jesus.

2. Trine Immersion.

Although Mack never argued that the particular mode was very important, he did maintain that immersion was the ultimate test of one's obedience to Christ.

3. Love Feast.

Along with baptism, the love feast was a mark of obedience. It is a rite in which only true believers are obligated and allowed to participate.

4. Disciplined Community.

Mack felt that if community was to develop, similarity of interests, faith, and common ties were essential, but not enough. A structure for equitable discipline and supportive help was also required. This was his purpose in espousing the ban and excommunication—to preserve the faith community.

5. Human Destiny

Hochmann, no doubt, had introduced to Mack the idea of ultimate restoration for all people. Mack could not believe that within the all-embracing love of God hell would be final for anybody.

Mack's pamphlet was written for Separatists of Schwarzenau, who were also being courted by the True Inspirationists. It is doubtful that it had much effect upon them, but it was useful in clarifying and strengthening the faith of those who were already Baptists. It was reprinted a number of times, and for several generations it was circulated in colonial America.

For the past two hundred years, however, few Brethren have known about Mack's publications and even fewer have read them. Yet both reveal Mack, the man, as a warm, sincere, earnest soul with deep religious sensitivity and compassion for human need. Although he tended at times to be somewhat legalistic, his searching spirit was not content to conform to patterns of life which had no religious meaning for him, and his courageous faith made it possible for him to chart new courses even though they were unpopular and perilous.

CHAPTER X

The Last Years at Schwarzenau
1715-1720

From 1715 to 1720, the Schwarzenau Baptist congregation grew very little. The spiritual momentum among the Separatists of Wittgenstein had shifted from the New Baptists to the aggressive Inspirationists. Having formed their first congregation in November 1714 at Himbach, by the summer of 1716, less than two years later, the Inspirationists had established ten strong congregations in Germany. The largest and most active was the Schwarzenau congregation.

Like the Brethren, the Inspirationists offered a strong communitarian fellowship and the complete service of the love feast. There was one very distinct difference, however, in their worship. The Inspirationists believed that direct revelations from God were received by their prophets (*Werkzeuge)*, whereas Mack and the baptists believed that God was revealed only through the person of Christ and the scriptures. Consequently, there was an emotional fervor in the Community of True Inspiration which the more orderly, serious-minded Baptists did not exhibit. Emotional intensity marked the Inspirationist style, sometimes prolonging their love feast for as much as sixteen hours.

Eberhard Gruber, who had very skillfully debated with Mack in 1713, was the leader of the Schwarzenau Inspirationists until his death in 1723. In 1717 his community was greatly enlarged by the arrival of forty refugees from Switzerland.

The Inspirationists were quite evangelistic, making many converts in Schwarzenau among the Separatists. They attempted to proselytize the New Baptists as well, attending their meetings and boldly delivering their own messages. One of them, a *Frau* Wagner, was so persistent that Mack was convinced she possessed an evil spirit. Mack attempted to exorcise that spirit by solemnly calling out: "I command you in the name of Jesus that you disappear, you unclean spirit!"[1] According to the Inspirationists, Mack's attempt failed, and *Frau* Wagner returned to testify at subsequent Baptist meetings with "inspired utterances"—presumably much to Alexander Mack's annoyance.

Ursula Meyer, an Inspirationist prophet, so opposed Mack that twice she called for his death. Believing that God would soon remove him from their presence, she cried scornfully: "I am pleased at your imminent fall, so that I can help those who sigh under your yoke."[2] She was disappointed. Mack did not die until 1735 in Pennsylvania. Ursula Meyer believed that Mack's legalistic institutionalism was a curse and a yoke upon the shoulders of his followers. She taunted him for worshiping the Bible. Mack denied the charges, protesting that direct revelation from God was not possible to her or any other Inspirationist prophet. Furthermore, Mack believed that her inspiration was from an evil spirit rather than from the Holy Spirit, for she did not prophesy in love.

Thwarted in their growth at both Marienborn and Schwarzenau, the New Baptists experienced their primary expansion in Krefeld. In 1716 a group of Separatists, both men and women, including their leader, John Lobach, were baptized in the Wupper River. These baptisms were still illegal, and six of the converts were duly arrested, sent to Düsseldorf for interrogation, and condemned to life imprisonment in the Jülich fortress.

In spite of such disturbances, the Krefeld congregation flourished until Christian Liebe returned from prison. A struggle for power between Naas and Liebe developed into a crisis in 1717, when John Häcker married the stepdaughter of a Mennonite minister. Christian Liebe insisted that Häcker be placed under the ban for marrying outside of the church. John Naas favored a milder rebuke. The turbulent controversy which developed over this issue became so bitter that John Naas withdrew from active participation in the life of the congregation. Many converts who had planned to be baptized chose not to do so. There was much turmoil that a sizable group decided to migrate to Pennsylvania. Peter Becker, though not of the leadership caliber of Liebe and Naas, had the ability to organize such an expedition as this one and took upon himself that responsibility. Since a group of twenty families were involved, the situation demanded a large amount of time and emotional dedication. In 1719, Becker's group sailed from a Dutch port on a vessel bound for Philadelphia.

Mack was unable to provide any significant help in the Krefeld situation, needing to devote most of his time to the problems in Schwarzenau, such as the crushing poverty of the Baptists. In the early part of 1719, however, Mack traveled to Krefeld, probably his last trip there. He crossed the mountains and went down the Rhine River to Jülich for a pastoral visit with the six Baptists imprisoned there. Although he made every effort to secure their release, it was primarily the influence of two Dutch Collegiants who made that possible on November 20, 1721.

The division within the leadership over Hacker's marriage, the strain caused by the imprisonment of six of its members, and the departure of Becker and twenty families for Pennsylvania all contributed to a decline in the size of and the enthusiasm within the group. Liebe left the congregation. John Naas and his family migrated to America (1733). As the New Baptists lost their sectarian zeal, some members joined the Mennonites while others withdrew completely from organized religion. Death took its inevitable toll, and under the influence of the Enlightenment, a period of antireligious and antisuperstitious emphasis on rational learning, the Krefeld congregation evolved into a small secular discussion group. Sometime between 1740 and 1760 the congregation disappeared.

Mack must have been disheartened over the early losses among these folk. He had invested so much of himself in this movement that its pain became his. He was, therefore, strongly attracted to the religious freedom to be found in William Penn's colony. He understandably followed news of Becker's migration with keen interest. Perhaps poverty was the only thing that prevented Mack and the Schwarzenau Baptists from following Becker's example.

In April 1719, Alexander Mack renewed his contract with Count Henry, who decreed that Mack "was not to be molested by anyone. He shall retain his freedom of conscience which I already granted him earlier."[3] It was evident that Mack had earned the respect of the count, who gave him special protection.

Hoping to publish a new hymnbook that would include hymns about baptism and the love feast, the Schwarzenau congregation had been compiling both appropriate Pietistic hymns and hymns they themselves had composed. This book was finally published by the Berleburg Press in 1720 under the title, *Geistreiches Gesangbuch*[4]

(Spiritual Songbook). Unfortunately, the hymnbooks were not released until after the New Baptists had left Schwarzenau, and only a few copies ever found their way to America.

The pressure of events finally compelled Mack to consider relocation. Financial problems were increasing. Those members who cut wood in Count Henry's forests for the charcoal-burning furnaces barely earned enough to survive. Over the years Mack had sold twenty-two pieces of personal property in Schriesheim, using the money for his family and the community, and was nearly destitute himself. In 1719 their poverty was so apparent that the Dutch Collegiants donated eight thousand guilders to help the "needy Schwarzenauers."[5]

By late 1719 there were ominous signs of increasing official opposition. Although they were still in favor with Count Henry, the New Baptists learned that a court decision had given considerable control over the forests of Wittgenstein to a younger brother, Count August David. Count Henry and Count August would become co-rulers of the Wittgenstein forests, giving Count August powerful influence over the economic life of the Baptist Brethren.[6]

Early in 1720, Count August David made an official complaint to the Imperial Supreme Court in Wetzlar about the settlers' damaging the forests and endangering the game. In truth, he was probably more perturbed by the settlers' religious persuasion than by environmental considerations, for Count August was known to be a very intolerant man.

Mack was concerned also when Count Henry, perhaps to placate his brother, expelled Christopher Seebach, a noted Separatist of Schwarzenau, from the territory because he had criticized the government and attacked the clergy.

In the spring of 1720, with conditions rapidly deteriorating, the New Baptists decided to leave Schwarzenau. Since migration to Pennsylvania was beyond their means, they looked to their previous benefactors, the Dutch Collegiants, for guidance. With their help, and with the hospitality of the Dutch Mennonites, a village in northwestern Holland was found for settlement, Surhuisterveen in Friesland.

Mack and his wife, Anna Margaret, had spent fourteen eventful years in Schwarzenau. As minister to the congregation, Mack had baptized about two hundred people, including his oldest son, John Valentine, in 1718. As one of his last official acts, he and his wife, with other members of the congregation, arose early one morning to baptize Mack's second son, John, at the same spot in the Eder River where the first Brethren baptisms had taken place.

Anna Margaret and the children prepared to leave. In 1720, John Valentine was nineteen, John was seventeen, Alexander, Jr., was seven, and Christina was six. A second daughter, Anna Margaret, had died in infancy. Demonstrating once again her quiet strength, Anna Margaret organized the packing for the move to Holland. She was a remarkable woman, holding the family together while her husband traveled, caring for itinerant Pietists in her home, welcoming the Baptists who gathered frequently in the Mack house for their meetings, and sharing her own bounty with the poor.

Mack sold their house to a distinguished Pietist from Ladenburg near Schriesheim, Christopher Sauer, who had been a resident of Schwarzenau for several years. Then he concentrated great effort in making preparation for the movement of forty families from Germany to Holland. Permits to leave Wittgenstein had to be bought from Count Henry. The Baptists felt warm gratitude to this considerate count, and they may have gone to his residence for a personal farewell. On his part, Henry was sincerely sorry to have these quiet, inoffensive Baptists leave his land. They had been dependable workers, and he was fond of them.

The day of departure arrived in May 1720. Roughly two hundred people parted from neighbors and friends to make this new journey of faith into an unknown land. Though he had been estranged from the Baptists for ten years, Hochmann, with his bountiful spirit of love, prayed for God's blessing to go with them. Their Swiss friend, Nicholas de Treytorrens, was sorry to see them go. Michael Eckerlin said a final goodbye to the Baptists, for, though he did not know it, he was to live less than a year.[7] Anticipation for the future and sadness at the break with the past were both present in this experience.

As the band of his followers rode or walked along the Eder River, Mack must have wondered at what God had wrought in his life. The future lay ahead—in Holland and in America.

Street in Surhuisterveen, Holland.

CHAPTER XI

Sojourn in Holland
1720-1729

The difficulties in moving two hundred people from Wittgenstein in Germany to northwestern Holland were staggering. According to Donald Durnbaugh, Mack, with his brethren and sisters, probably

> . . . took the local road to Siegen where they could meet the main overland route to Köln. Here they could board boats which plied the Rhine River, taking them into the low countries, where they likely disembarked at Nÿmegen for the trek north to Friesland.[1]

After several weeks of travel, the weary group arrived at Surhuisterveen, where they were warmly welcomed by hospitable Dutch Mennonites. Surhuisterveen had been founded around 1600 by Mennonites who worked the peat bogs, digging and shipping the peat for fuel. It was located midway between two larger towns, Groningen and Leeuwarden, both of which had strong Mennonite congregations and groups of Collegiants. Just twenty miles from the North Sea, Surhuisterveen was only a few feet above sea level. Much of its surrounding land was below sea level, marshy and green.

This Mennonite community had a Waterlander church background, which indicated that it was more liberally oriented than the Dutch Mennonites in southern Holland. They may have opened their worship services and communion rites to Mack and the New Baptists, as they did to the Collegiants. However, since Mennonites did not practice baptism by immersion, the New Baptists declined participation in communion.

Soon after their arrival, Mack's people found work digging peat. Because peat was cheap and readily available, they used it to build themselves small houses, set halfway below ground level according to the custom of that area. Mack's house, built across the street from the Mennonite parsonage, was large enough to accommodate congregational gatherings.

Wopke Rommerts was the Mennonite lay preacher during this time. He was quite friendly toward these new settlers, and may have been partially responsible, along with the Collegiants, for the New Baptists' decision to settle in Surhuisterveen.

Immersion had been a live issue for Mennonites in northern Germany and Holland for many years. To them, the German Baptists' attitudes were not new. In 1650 a portion of the Hamburg Mennonite church had withdrawn from the congregation over immersion, though continuing to meet in the same church building. They called themselves *"Dompelaars,"* which was the name by which the German Baptists were also known in Holland. By 1708 the Hamburg *Dompelaars* were numerous enough to construct their own church building.[2]

With the encouragement of Mennonites in northern Germany and the Collegiants, several Mennonite congregations in Holland had permitted the practice of immersion for at least a generation. In 1715 the Leeuwarden congregation had adopted immersion, but a great deal of controversy resulted. By 1720 the immersionists were forced out of the congregation. Five years later they were reinstated, and a baptistry was even built in the church.[3]

As early as 1688, in the Groningen Mennonite church, twenty miles east of Surhuisterveen, a minister had been excommunicated for advocating immersion. The Surhuisterveen Mennonites, though occasionally permitting immersion, generally practiced pouring. For them, apparently, immersion was not a controversial issue.

Although the New Baptists were pleased with the religious freedom and the friendly welcome they had found in Holland, one feature of Dutch life really disturbed them. To see their Dutch neighbors gliding effortlessly on skates over the frozen ponds and canals was so shocking that they denounced ice-skating as the work of the devil. If the Baptists were at all like other immigrants to Holland, however, within a short time they too had adopted this new mode of transportation. One contribution which the German Baptists made to the Dutch was the introduction of potatoes.

In September 1720 a double tragedy struck Mack and his community. His dearly beloved wife of nineteen years died unexpectedly,[4] a tragedy followed by the death of his six-year-old daughter, Christina, one week later. James Quinter wrote in 1860 that Anna Margaret Mack "found in death what she and her husband had sought in vain for on earth, a calm retreat from the storm of persecution."[5] Quinter described Mack's wife as a meek and virtuous woman. Her death was a painfully grave blow to Mack, for Anna Margaret's quiet strength and fortitude had been a major support to him through the years. Needing to care for his three sons, provide spiritual leadership to his congregation in a strange land, help meet the economic needs of his people, and proclaim his faith according to his calling, Mack could spend little time mourning.

In late 1720, Mack received word that Peter Becker and his party had landed safely in Philadelphia. This was triumphant news! Unfortunately, the differences which had originally precipitated the migration from Krefeld erupted again on board ship. So, when the New Baptists arrived in Pennsylvania, families scattered in different directions. Peter Becker, John Gumre, and several others chose to settle in Germantown. The remainder moved farther west to Oley and Falckner's Swamp, where Mennonites had already settled. Becker set up a weaving business. A heavy demand for woven goods in the colonies helped make his business prosper in a few short months. Needing help, he engaged an apprentice for one year, a young man named Conrad Beissel.

Mack must have recognized the name when he heard this news from the New World, for Beissel had been an ardent Pietist in Heidelberg and a close associate of Haller. In 1718, two years before Mack's departure, Beissel had arrived in Schwarzenau as a member of the Community of True Inspiration. Breaking with the Inspirationists, Beissel had sailed for Boston in 1720. Finding very few German immigrants there, he moved on to Germantown, where he developed a close friendship with Peter Becker. Both men were deeply spiritual. Beissel's intense religious fervor may have prompted Becker to seek Mack's advice concerning the lack of religious activity among the Baptists in the New World. Following his apprenticeship, Beissel chose to withdraw from society and live as a contemplative in the forested area of Conestoga near Lancaster.

Mack was sorry to hear that Old World dissension had been carried to the New. Although he regretted that the Brethren were not gathering regularly for worship, he was encouraged by Becker's concern and initiative. Mack did not feel administratively responsible for moderating the affairs of either Krefeld or Germantown, for he did not think of himself as the head of a denomination. He considered the Baptist movement as a group of congregations, each one of which was seeking to develop a New Testament pattern of life. With that basic understanding, Mack advised Becker to minister to the scattered Brethren in Pennsylvania and to organize a congregation of believers if possible.

Meanwhile, Mack was kept busy with his own people's needs. He preached regularly at their worship services, officiated at funerals, attended to their material and spiritual needs, and worked with his sons in the peat bogs when work was available. Mack was no longer a wealthy man, for the little which had remained of his plenty had been used for the move to Holland, and work in the bogs was neither lucrative nor steady.

Mack was not paid for his services to the congregation. This was his spiritual calling, his "gift" to be used for the community. There were two types of ministry among the German Baptists: the lay preacher and the bishop *(Vorsteher)*. Each congregation had one or more lay ministers who preached, taught, and helped administer communion. These lay preachers were chosen by election or consensus. The *Vorsteher,* who was called to oversee the affairs of the whole congregation, was ordained. Alexander Mack was the bishop of the Surhuisterveen congregation, working in a pattern which may represent Mennonite influence. Peter Becker became the bishop of Germantown. How Becker was ordained, though, remains a mystery to church historians. Perhaps he felt that the commission laid upon him by Mack's letters constituted ordination. The responsibilities of bishops were varied—marriages, baptisms, funerals, communion.

In early 1721, Mack baptized a young Dutch convert, John Juriens, who was probably a Mennonite. The service was held at a large pond in the Kortwalde, several miles east of Surhuisterveen. John Juriens had announced his intention to marry Anna Catherine Kipping, the daughter of John and Joanna Kipping, who were two of the original eight baptized at Schwarzenau.

When John and Anna Catherine came to Mack to announce their plans, Mack had a new decision to make. It was customary in both the Dutch Reformed and the Mennonite churches to have engaged couples proclaim their "intentions" three times publicly before the wedding. Mack could have used either of these churches as a vehicle to record the bans. He decided not to do this. Not wishing to endanger or compromise the autonomy of the New Baptist community, he decided instead to go with the engaged couple on April 28, 1721, to a local government official where the first marriage proclamation was duly recorded in the secular records. A week later he appeared with them for the second proclamation. On May 19, they appeared for the third time, as was required by custom, and on this occasion Mack married them in the presence of the government official and his secretary, who served as witnesses. This was a decided break with Dutch tradition.

Although Mack did not feel administratively responsible for the affairs of other congregations, he did feel a kindly interest in their lives. His sympathy for the Brethren imprisoned at Jülich, his concern for the divisive factions developing in the congregation at Krefeld, and his desire to receive news from his friends and fellow workers left behind in Schwarzenau spread his interest far beyond Friesland. So he was deeply grieved when the unexpected news came that Ernest Christopher Hochmann had died on January 12, 1721, in Schwarzenau. Although they had been estranged for years, Mack felt a debt of gratitude to this man who had once been his closest friend and mentor. It was Hochmann who had encouraged Mack in his quest for religious freedom to separate from the German Reformed Church. It was Hochmann who had participated in many of the Pietist meetings which had helped shape Mack's beliefs. It was Hochmann's letter from the Nürnberg jail which had encouraged Mack to make that eventful decision to conduct the first baptismal service in the Eder River.

No public mourning, no elaborate ceremonies, no tributes from royalty or bishops of the church accompanied Hochmann's passing. When Count Zinzendorf visited Schwarzenau in 1730, he observed that Hochmann's presence and influence had completely diminished and that there was no trace left of his past religious activity or his dynamic personality. He left no church to honor him; he left no enduring school of thought; he left no band of followers, no estate, no books or learned articles. However, Hochmann was not forgotten by the Brethren in Surhuisterveen or in Pennsylvania. Among them he was remembered through his Detmold Confession of Faith, a confession the Brethren frequently studied and repeatedly published.

Mack's feelings toward Hochmann were mixed. Mack had gradually diverged from Hochmann's emphasis on freedom and inclusive love and had moved toward a sectarian, institutional position.

Mack felt this was essential in order to maintain the "purity" of the faith and the stability of the Christian community. Mack probably never rid himself of feeling Hochmann's strong disapproval for his taking a strict stand on believers' baptism, closed communion, and church discipline for the unruly.

Not all of the New Baptists were pleased with Mack's strict position. It is evident that soon after their arrival in Holland some divisiveness and bad feeling developed in the congregation. A situation similar to that in Krefeld arose. In an open meeting, George Grebe, one of the original eight, denounced Mack saying, "You and all of yours are dead and have died to the life of God."[6] Grebe took a position similar to that held earlier by John Naas and Ernest Hochmann, that inclusive love was more important than legalism. Grebe was quite critical of Mack's rigidity, quoting, "The letter killeth, but the spirit giveth life."

The irony of this situation must have been apparent to Mack. In his youth he had assaulted a rigidly entrenched and unresponsive church in the same way. Now he was the conservator of an institution and was himself being assaulted. The majority, however, supported Mack and seemed to have had genuine affection, admiration, and gratitude for what he had done in their behalf.

During this period, the life of the congregation was reinvigorated by the arrival of William Knepper, one of the Solingen Brethren who had been imprisoned at Jülich. He brought the welcome news that all of the prisoners had been set free. Soon after his arrival in Surhuisterveen, he became engaged to a young Dutch woman, Veronica Bloom. Since Veronica had been baptized by sprinkling or pouring, she asked Mack to baptize her again by immersion, in preparation for their marriage. This service was performed in the Kortwalde pond, and on February 22, 1723, Mack married them in a New Baptist ceremony.

In the same year, Mack received word from the New World that Peter Becker and two other Brethren had visited "all their Brethren scattered throughout the land,"[7] meeting good response wherever they went. Upon their return, weekly meetings were held for the Germantown Baptists, alternating between Peter Becker's home and John Gumre's. When a rumor that Christian Liebe from Krefeld was arriving at Philadelphia spread among the various settlements, a number of persons from the Coventry area went to the port to meet him. When he did not appear, they visited the Germantown Baptists. After attending several meetings, six persons from this group requested baptism. This precipitated the hasty organization of the German-town congregation.

On Christmas morning, 1723, seventeen Brethren met in the Becker home to organize the Germantown congregation formally with Peter Becker as its bishop. After an appropriate devotional serv-ice with the six applicants for baptism, this small group filed reverent-ly down an old Indian trail to the Wissahickon Creek, one and one-half miles from the Becker house. After singing Mack's hymn, "Count the Cost," and reading from Luke 14, Becker immersed each of the postulants three times in the icy stream.

Following the baptisms, they went to the home of John Gumre, where, as evening fell, the Brethren celebrated their first love feast in the New World.

Since mail was slow, Mack probably did not hear of these events until the summer of 1724. Mail from the New World took from three to six months to be delivered, but later letters informed Mack of more baptisms and of a religious "awakening" with "remarkable man-ifestations" of the Spirit. The receipt of such news was an occasion of great joy and encouragement to the Surhuisterveen Baptists.

Though Mack was excited by news from the New World, his chief obligations continued to be with the welfare of his own congre-gation. He performed two weddings in 1724: that of John Henry Kalcklöser and Anna Flys Layen, a young Dutch woman, and that of Jacob Bossert and Susan Keymen. Jacob Bossert's parents had first entertained Mack at Himbach, and had migrated with him to Holland. Susan was also from the German provinces. Both of these young couples, deeply loyal to Mack, later migrated with him to Ger-mantown.

Occasionally, visitors attended the New Baptist meetings: Collegiants interested in the growth of the immersionist movement, or Mennonites who favored immersion. Infrequently, New Baptists from other areas joined them in worship. An elderly gentleman named Partel Jürgen Petersen, from Altona in northern Germany, made the long journey to Surhuisterveen several times to worship with Mack and the others. The congregation welcomed his visits, and Mack learned to know him quite well.

Petersen had been baptized into the Lutheran Church as an in-fant. His childhood had not been an easy one, and he had never learned to read or write. Although by trade a fisherman, he had spent some time as a soldier in the German army. However, because his conscience troubled him, he experienced a Pietistic conversion. Applying for, and receiving, release from his duties as a soldier, he returned home determined to lead a new life. He attended church regularly, but his spiritual hunger was not filled. He bought a New Testament, but could not read it. With the help of schoolchildren after school hours, he mastered reading. Within two weeks he was able to read his New Testament.

Impressed by the New Testament baptisms, he inquired of knowledgeable people if there were any Christians who baptized in this fashion. He was told of the New Baptists at Krefeld. Immediately, in the middle of winter, he went in search of this congregation and persuaded its minister to baptize him on the day of his arrival. The creek was frozen, but Petersen insisted that the minister break the ice and proceed.

In writing about Petersen years later, Alexander Mack, Jr., said that he

> . . . went home happily, and led a devout life until his natural death. He lived to be almost ninety years of age. This man often visited us in Friesland, and therefore I learned to know him very well. I loved him dearly, and he loved me.[8]

In 1722 the Mennonite minister, Wopke Rommerts of Surhuisterveen, died. His successor, Jan Thomas, was very liberal in his thought, with pronounced Socinian views which raised questions about the Trinity. Socinianism was illegal in Friesland, and for a time Jan Thomas had been suspended from the ministry by the provincial government. Thomas was not alone on this issue. Many Waterlander ministers were receptive to such ideas, leaning toward a kind of unitarianism.

In 1722 Freisland had become so alarmed by the prevalence of Socinian views that the government drew up a confession specifically repudiating Socinianism and required all Mennonite pastors to sign it. If Jan Thomas signed it, he must, however, have had some mental reservation. He was finally allowed to resume preaching; in 1722 he moved to Surhuisterveen, where he served the Mennonite church until his death in 1744.

Thomas expressed his liberal orientation by closely associating with the Collegiants. During his ministry, his church was composed of approximately one hundred thirty members—a rather large congregation compared to other rural Mennonite churches in northern Holland at that time. Apparently Thomas never allowed his personal attitudes to become an issue of controversy, and he served the church for twenty-two years.

In 1725, Mack heard more of the remarkable religious revival taking place in Pennsylvania. During the fall of 1724, Peter Becker, with fourteen others to assist him, had converted and baptized many new believers at a number of pioneer settlements. On November 7, they organized a second congregation of German Baptists at Coventry, choosing Martin Urner as its preacher and Peter Becker as its bishop.

These evangelists then pressed on to Conestoga, enlisting Conrad Beissel's support in their efforts. According to the *Ephrata Chronicle,* "extraordinary revival powers were manifested" in these meetings with six persons receiving baptism in the Pequea Creek. Beissel watched the baptisms with rapt intensity. Although he wanted to be baptized, he did not want to submit himself to baptism by Peter Becker, for he considered Becker his spiritual inferior. Yet, deeply troubled that he had never been baptized in the "Apostolic fashion," he "came down from his spiritual pride, humbled himself before his friend, Peter Becker, and was baptized by him . . . Apostolic-wise."[9]

Subsequently, a congregation was formed with Beissel as its minister and Becker as its bishop. To the consternation of the Germantown Baptists, however, Beissel's congregation kept Saturday as their holy day. They argued that this was biblical, and that certainly Alexander Mack would look favorably upon its practice. There is no evidence, though, that Mack had any such inclination. It is possible that the matter had been discussed by the Schwarzenau Baptists when they first established their mode and practice. Beissel felt that their rejection of the Sabbath had been due to a lack of courage and conviction. Although Mack did not consider it wrong to observe the seventh day, it was contrary to his own basic theology to establish an Old Testament practice as a requirement for fellowship. The Germantown Baptists took much the same view as did Mack. They were fearful, however, that Beissel might attempt to impose his views on them.

So much controversy developed between the Conestoga Baptists on the one side and the Coventry and Germantown Baptists on the other, that Christopher Sauer was compelled to observe that the "Brethren have erected a fence around themselves; they admit and expell, and are jealous of and quarrelsome with others."[10]

During 1725, Mack performed a number of baptisms and at least three marriages in Holland. The first marriage was that of his second son, John, twenty-one, whom he married to Joanna (Anna) Margaret Süderein from Germany on February 26. John was an apprenticed weaver and later worked at his trade in Pennsylvania. John and Anna Margaret soon added two girls to the Mack family, Anna Margaret and Phillipine, both born in Holland and destined to take the long eventful voyage to the New World a few years later.

The second marriage was performed in March for Johannes Lodewyck Beinum, a Hollander, and Ann Senebecken from Germany. This couple chose to remain in Holland when the others emigrated.

In April, Mack performed a third marriage, that of Christian Schneider and Susan Macking, both from Germany. This was the last of seven recorded marriages performed by Mack in Surhuisterveen. Five of these young couples migrated with Mack to the New World.

Although the Baptist community rejoiced with these young couples at their weddings, their joy was tinged with anxiety. The economic situation in their community was precarious. Income from the peat fields was often insufficient to purchase adequate food supplies. Since Mack had used all of his inheritance, there were no emergency reserves. There were periods of real hunger and near-starvation. Hearing of their plight, the Dutch Collegiants again responded readily. Adrian Pauw, a prominent Collegiant citizen and wealthy burgher of Heemstede, apparently gave generously toward their support. Pauw had been a Dutch nobleman and a member of the Estates General, but upon his conversion in 1704, he had resigned from his public office to lead "a secluded life, hidden in Christ in God."[11]

Years later, Alexander Mack, Jr., wrote warmly of the Collegiants, remembering the concern and generosity they had shown the German Baptists. Alexander Mack treated them as "Brethren," welcoming them on occasion to the Baptist worship services and perhaps even to their love feasts. The Collegiants did not submit to "Brethren baptism," since they had already been immersed according to Collegiant tradition.

In 1727, Mack's poverty was relieved, at least for a while. John Valentine Kling, Mack's father-in-law, who had died in 1714, had bequeathed a sizable inheritance to Mack. Reluctant to leave his congregation, or perhaps forbidden to return to Schriesheim, Mack sent his three sons to settle the Kling estate.

Although this inheritance provided welcome relief, Mack was becoming increasingly certain that the German Baptists faced a very insecure future in Surhuisterveen. Peat bogs are soon depleted and marshes are quickly drained for farmland. Since the land belonged to Mennonite and Dutch Reformed families, the Baptists would be able to work only as farmhands at very low wages. This dismal prospect contrasted sharply with the reports Mack received from the New World describing abundant work opportunities, cheap land, and building materials.

In 1724, John Käsebier of Schwarzenau had sailed with a group of German emigrants to Philadelphia. Shortly after his arrival, he sent a lengthy letter back to Count Casimir in Berleburg, describing the fertile countryside. Mack may not have seen Käsebier's letter, but he had received other letters equally encouraging.

Sheltered by John Gumre, Käsebier wrote this letter on November 7:

> As far as this country is concerned, it is a precious land with the finest wheat, as well as unusual corn, fine broom corn, maize, and white beets of such quality as I never saw in Germany. . . . There are apples in great quantities from trees which grow up wild without being grafted. . . . Many trees are full of apples which are frozen because there is a shortage of workers.

> The man in our house, John Gumre, came to this country in 1719 and did not bring much with him. Now he has property worth at least one thousand Florins, three horses, cows and sheep, hens and sows.

> The trees which grow in the forests are cedar, two kinds of nut trees, chestnut and many young oaks. It is, however, so easy to be cleared that it is hard to believe. Deer, rabbits . . . pheasants, wild partridge, and pigeons are plentiful, and all can be shot without limit.[12]

With such promise and hope for the future, Käsebier's death a few weeks after writing the letter saddened Mack and the whole Baptist community.

In 1724, Mack's friend from Schwarzenau, Christopher Sauer, wrote glowingly to his European friends of the "well-blessed land" of Pennsylvania. Sauer reported that an artisan without debts could purchase a property of one hundred acres within two or three years, including a "soundly built stone house."[13]

Although Mack was deeply grateful to the Dutch for the freedom of conscience which the New Baptists enjoyed in Friesland, he knew that their mode of baptism was still technically illegal. As early as 1662 a law had been passed prohibiting immersion. In 1686 this law was renewed. This illegality, along with the bleak economic future the Baptists faced in Friesland, were deep concerns for Mack. Even though Mack had never been molested by the Dutch civil authorities, he could not be sure about the future. In spite of the friendship shown the Baptists by Jan Thomas and others in his congregation, some of the Dutch Mennonites felt quite hostile toward the immersionists. Shortly before Mack's arrival, some leaders in the Leeuwarden Mennonite congregation had enlisted the help of civil authorities to stamp out the practice of immersion in their community.

In contrast to the uneasy acceptance in Friesland, reports from Pennsylvania seemed extremely attractive. Under the tolerant rule of Pennsylvania's Quakers, the German Baptists had complete religious freedom, with no legal threats hanging over their heads. One of the Pennsylvania Brethren reported that their freedom was indescribable. In one of Christopher Sauer's letters, he reported that freedom of religion was so pervasive that "the children of God . . . are secure from outward persecution."[14]

To Alexander Mack, an especially appealing feature of Pennsylvania's freedom was the church's opportunity to conduct evangelistic work openly. In Friesland, there were many limitations and frustrations. The Frisian language, although related to German, was generally incomprehensible to the New Baptists. With this language barrier, the German Baptists had made few converts in the nine years they had lived in Surhuisterveen. Except for a few Dutch young people who had married Baptists, the membership had grown very little, and more likely had declined. Some had married outside the faith, and some, perhaps, had returned to Germany. About two hundred people had migrated from Germany to Holland in 1720. About one hundred eighteen migrated to America in 1729. Mack was astute enough to recognize that a significant decline in membership in less than a decade promised little future for a German Baptist congregation in Holland.

After much prayer and congregational discussion, the decision to migrate to America was made. What an extraordinary, courageous action! It was not taken easily or made hastily. The group was quite aware of death at sea, shipwrecks, and unknown perils. Although the cost of such a trip was almost forbidding, with faith they made plans and looked forward to a new home in a new land.

Peter Becker may have been the deciding factor for Mack when he wrote expressing a real need for Mack to come to Pennsylvania to provide leadership for the German Baptists there. By 1728 the situation in the Pennsylvania churches had changed. Conrad Beissel, the lay preacher at Conestoga, had repudiated Peter Becker's leadership as bishop, and had pronounced a ban against all of the Germantown Baptists and those at Coventry (and elsewhere) who were loyal to them and their traditions. The Germantown Brethren reciprocated. Beissel felt compelled to break with the Brethren; so he "gave their baptism" back to them by going into the water and being immersed three times "backward." The irony in Beissel's defection was his insistence that he was being faithful to the original Baptist movement at Schwarzenau.

Not all of the Surhuisterveen Baptists chose to go with Mack to the New World. George Grebe and his wife, in spite of their long relationship, did not. In those families where German Baptist women had intermarried with Dutch citizens, there was reluctance to leave Holland. A few families probably chose to return to friends and relatives in Germany. A very few may have remained in Surhuisterveen.

In the spring of 1729, the months of planning for migration to America came to a climax. About thirty families sold everything except the few possessions they were able to pack in portable chests and bade farewell to Mennonite and Collegiant friends. Horse-drawn wagons may have carried the infirm, the provisions, and the heavy chests, while the rest of the group walked to the port of Rotterdam, a distance of one hundred twenty-five miles. If money was available, they were able to travel most of the way by canal boat.

In Rotterdam, the Baptists were met by the De Koker family, and other Collegiants, who helped care for the group until a suitable ship was engaged. It was Mack's responsibility to make arrangements for a ship and to purchase adequate provisions. Although the ship's captain provided food on the passage, shipboard fare was minimal and monotonous. Reports from other voyagers indicated that rice, barley, peas, small amounts of cheese, and almost inedible salted meat were the basic supplies. Each of the families, wishing to supplement this fare, planned to carry dried apples, pears, and plums, a vat of mustard, a bottle of brandy, and, if possible, a whole ham. Families were required to furnish their own bedding and pillows. They were encouraged to fill all empty spaces in their chests with items in great demand in the New World, such as needles, pins, and cloth.

If money was not available for passage, the captain would willingly provide transportation in exchange for an agreement of indenture to some family in America to work for them free of charge for a period of time, ranging from six months to several years. When the ship docked in Philadelphia, the captain then exchanged this agreement, and the person who signed it, with the host family for the cost of passage. An indentured immigrant received food and shelter, and at the conclusion of his service a new suit of clothes with a sum of money to help him get started. Such immigrants were expected to work diligently and cause their hosts no trouble. It is not likely, however, that many of the Brethren, if any, on this voyage were indentured, for the Germantown Baptists were able and willing to help any who were in need.

Finally, in the latter part of June 1729, Mack with his three sons and the rest of the Brethren boarded a ship called the *Allen*. Its captain was Master James Craigie, a British seaman. The *Allen* could scarcely be called a ship; it was not as large as the ferry boats which ply the waters between New York City and Staten Island. Since passengers were more valuable than cargo, Captain Craigie crowded as many persons on board as was possible. Sailing conditions during this period of colonization were so bad that a whole family might be allowed a space of only three by six feet.

Conditions aboard the *Allen* are unrecorded, but it was most likely overcrowded, unclean, and uncomfortable. So far as is known, this was the only voyage the *Allen* ever made to the New World; and it was apparently Craigie's first command across the Atlantic.

About the first day of July, the *Allen* set sail from Rotterdam, the chief port of German emigration. Between 1727 and 1775, three hundred twenty-four ships carried German migrants to Philadelphia. Most of these voyages originated in Rotterdam, Holland's busiest port.

After crossing the turbulent English Channel, the *Allen* docked for several days at Cowes on the Isle of Wight, where water, provisions, and additional passengers were taken on board.

On July 7, 1729, the tiny vessel set out to cross the vast Atlantic. With favorable winds and good weather, some ships made the voyage to Philadelphia in seven weeks. It took the Allen ten. Sometimes it encountered calm, balmy weather when no progress could be made.

Artist's portrayal of an 18th century sailing ship.
Maritime Museum, Rotterdam

At other times, occasional severe summer storms would blow it off course. Everyone, including the crew, huddled below deck during these storms. Planks had to be lashed to the portholes to block out the raging water; but when storms were unusually violent, everyone was soaked to the skin in spite of the obstructing planks. Seasickness was rampant during stormy weather.

Andrew Boni became so discouraged by the hardships endured on the *Allen* that he later wrote back to a cousin in Europe: "I can hardly encourage someone to come because of the great, long, and difficult journey."[15] Illnesses, dirty clothes and bodies, foul odors, lice and other vermin and unpalatable drinking water were a few of the difficult aspects of this move to America.

Almost every voyage had its share of deaths. Usually children and the elderly were the first to die. There are no records of deaths on the *Allen*, but it is reasonable to assume that there were some, for Brumbaugh in his *History of the Brethren* wrote that it was a tempestuous and perilous voyage. Upon their arrival in Philadelphia, four passengers were so sick that the official list recorded in the courthouse mentioned their illnesses.[16]

Early in September, after weeks of hardship and waning strength, the Brethren were tremendously reassured when they spotted land. Prayers of thanksgiving and hymns of praise must have filled the air as the tiny *Allen* entered the broad, twenty-five-mile sweep of Delaware Bay.

Somewhere between the ocean and the Delaware River, the *Allen* stopped to take on board a local pilot to navigate the ship up-river to the port of Philadelphia. A physician was also taken aboard to examine the passengers for infectious diseases.

The last portion of the trip was frustratingly slow, lasting perhaps more than a week. From a distance, the passengers could see the stately buildings, the tall church spires, and the busy port of the largest city in the colonies. From December 1729 to March 1732, one hundred eighty-nine ships entered this port. A bustling city of commerce, Philadelphia was also the provincial capital of Pennsylvania, with a population of approximately twenty thousand people.

Brethren from Germantown, Coventry, and Conestoga came to Philadelphia to welcome their weary European brothers and sisters. Peter Becker undoubtedly led this delegation. Some were young, some old. Some had become relatively rich in the New World. Others had chosen to live lives of poverty. Some had known Mack in Europe. Others came out of eagerness to meet this highly respected leader of their faith.

Mack was the first to step off the ship and to be greeted by Peter Becker with the kiss of charity practiced by the Brethren from their beginning. John Mack and his family followed, then Valentine and Alexander, Jr., Andrew Boni and his wife, with John Kipping and his wife, all members of the original eight, followed. Other families who eagerly set foot on land were the Kalcklösers, Schneiders, Leslies, Kiessels, Kresses, and Bosserts. Altogether there were thirty family units.

Before leaving for Germantown, the newly arrived Baptists had to fulfill provincial council law. The names of all who had survived the trip had to be recorded with Captain Craigie. His record shows that sixty-four males and fifty-eight females, with five male children under fifteen, arrived on the *Allen*. Several of the passengers were non-Brethren. This list was certified on Captain Craigie's oath and submitted to the provincial government.

Every adult male German was also required to sign a pledge of allegiance to the British king. Mack and the other men went to the courthouse on September 15, where they signed the following pledge of loyalty:

> We Subscribers, Natives and Late Inhabitants of the Palatinate upon the Rhine and places adjacent, having transported ourselves, and families into this Province of Pensilvania, a Colony subject to the Crown of Great Britain, in Hopes and Expectation of finding a Retreat and peaceable Settlement therein, Do solemnly promise and Engage that We will be faithful and bear true Allegiance to his present MAJESTY KING GEORGE THE SECOND, and his Successors, Kings of Great Britain, and will be faithful to the Proprietor of this Province; and that we will demean ourselves peaceably to all this said Majestie's subjects, and strictly observe and conform to the Laws of England and of this Province, to the utmost of our Power and best of our understanding.[17]

Mack could not understand English; so he listened very carefuly as the pledge was interpreted to him. Out of respect for the many Mennonite and Baptist immigrants, this pledge was not written as an oath. Mack signed it, followed by his three sons and all the other male adults. Fifteen of these Brethren were illiterate and signed with initials or crosses.

The state further required that all immigrants sign a pledge of abjuration, never to support any pretender to the British throne.

Again Mack and his sons signed first as an example to the others.

Finally, they were free to go along with the other Brethren up the "Great Road" to Peter Becker's house. This was a seven-mile trip to a settlement called Beggarstown, north of Germantown. After great rejoicing and feasting, the new immigrants were distributed among the homes of the Germantown Baptist families.

Mack went to bed in the New World with gratitude in his heart for a safe journey and arrival, but with troubled concern over Beissel and the perplexing situation in Conestoga.

CHAPTER XII

The Years in Germantown
1729-1735

For these new German Baptist immigrants, the first years in Germantown were intensely fulfilling. Years of harassment and rejection experienced in Europe made the accepting love of the Germantown Brethren an incomparable blessing. They were treated as welcome additions to the Germantown congregation and as strong support for the Baptists in their struggle against Beissel. To be wanted and loved was a delightful experience.

Peter Becker was especially pleased for Mack's solid support. When the Conestoga congregation divided in 1728, half of its people followed Beissel, while the other half remained loyal to the Germantown church. Becker, as the bishop of the Germantown, Coventry, and Conestoga congregations, had carried the primary burden of the broken fellowship. Shortly after his arrival, Mack assumed leadership at Germantown and made a visit to Coventry, where he installed Martin Urner as *Vorsteher,* or bishop. This freed Becker to assume undivided responsibility for the congregation at Conestoga.

There is no reported indication of resentment between the two men over this transition in leadership. Mack and Becker respected each other. Though Becker's views on church discipline were more moderate than Mack's, both men genuinely loved the church they served, and in that love they found unity.

Mack performed his pastoral duties eagerly, happy in his freedom to practice his faith without restraint. The congregation responded to his leadership with Pietistic enthusiasm. From 1730 to 1735, the Germantown church grew steadily, becoming a stable congregation with few internal problems.

With Mack's arrival, and the addition of many families to their services, the homes of John Gumre and Peter Becker became inadequate meeting places. When weather permitted, the worshipers met in an open field; or in inclement weather in a barn. Occasionally they simply canceled services, especially in the winter.

One of Mack's most immediate problems was economic. He and his two unmarried sons, John Valentine and Sander (Alexander, Jr.), were living with one of the host families until they could build a house of their own. Being hard-working, responsible men, they wanted to earn their own way as soon as possible and repay those families who had made contributions to their passage on the *Allen.*

Knowing the miller's trade best, Mack may have considered becoming a miller. However, there was already one gristmill operating in the area, the Townsend mill. Richard Townsend, an English millwright, had come to Pennsylvania with William Penn on the *Welcome* in 1683. His business, located one mile east of Germantown, was flourishing. Although Mack may have worked temporarily at this mill, it is more probable that he assisted his sons in the weaving business they had established. It is likely that if Mack's responsibilities to the church became heavy, his sons supported him.

John Mack had learned the weaving trade in Holland. He was able to go to work immediately, and soon had a prosperous business. In October 1730, he purchased a half-acre of land on the main street of Germantown from Peter Shoemaker and wife. By 1734, he had bought two more acres of land in Germantown and eighteen acres in Roxborough. John Mack and his family remained in Germantown until 1751, when they moved to a location near Waynesboro, Pennsylvania. There he became an active leader in the German Baptist churches of that area.

Since there was great demand for items like stockings, caps, and woven fabric, it was not difficult to become established as a weaver. Mack's unmarried sons had learned the trade either from their brother John or their friend, Peter Becker. Sander continued as a weaver for the rest of his life, providing adequately for his family but never accumulating wealth. John Valentine, upon the death of his father, withdrew from the business and entered the Ephrata community for life.

Mack's most perplexing problem continued to be the split between the Germantown Brethren and the Conestoga Brethren who followed Beissel. In 1728, Beissel had published a tract which used the same format as Mack's *Rights and Ordinances,* a dialog between father and son. As Mack had argued for immersion, Beissel argued for keeping the Sabbath holy. According to Julius Sachse, the historian of early Pennsylvania, this booklet "caused a great sensation among the Germans in the rural districts."[1] In 1729, the booklet was translated into English by Michael Wohlfahrt, one of Beissel's intimate and devoted followers. Shortly before Mack's arrival, Brother Joel (Peter Bucher) confronted the Germantown Brethren at one of their meetings, pronouncing judgment upon them and denouncing Peter Becker to his face. Mack read Beissel's pamphlet, heard of Brother Joel's accusations, and listened with great sadness to accounts of Beissel's tirades against the Germantown Brethren. Even in the New World, with its wealth of opportunity and freedom, his dream for a Christian community of caring love was difficult to achieve.

Beissel's pervasive influence was felt even by the Pennsylvania Quakers. Soon after Mack's arrival, he learned of Michael Wohlfahrt's interference at a Quaker meeting in Philadelphia. Wohlfahrt had attended a service, listened at length to a Quaker woman who was speaking, and, growing impatient, had rudely interrupted her to make his own speech—exhorting the Quakers to keep the Sabbath holy. Later, he held an open-air meeting on the courthouse steps proclaiming the necessity for obedience to the fourth commandment. The Quakers were understandably irritated by Wohlfahrt's behavior and were not overjoyed to learn that his sermon had been published in both German and English for distribution in the colony.

Mack repeatedly attempted to meet Beissel, hoping to establish a reconciliation between the two groups of Brethren. Loathe to engage in extended doctrinal controversy, which he felt had caused the established churches of Europe to lose their love of God, Mack pondered his approach to Beissel. On his part, Beissel deliberately avoided meeting Mack. He did not want to encourage any threat to his own religious leadership—especially from the "venerable patriarch," Mack.

The Germantown Baptists could not attend Wohlfahrt's meetings in Philadelphia, since each group of Brethren had put the other group under the ban. However, Benjamin Franklin did attend one of Wohlfahrt's open-air meetings at the courthouse, not so much because of his interest in Wohlfahrt's Sabbatarian views, but because of a business interest in publishing Beissel's tracts and books.

In 1730, Franklin published his first book for Beissel. It was a small book—a book of poems and proverbs, which may very well have been the very first volume published by the Franklin press. In this thirty-two-page booklet, Beissel had expressed himself through ninety-nine moralistic, practical proverbs with mystical overtones, and a series of poems. Beissel's first major commission to Franklin was the 1730 publication of a hymnbook which had sixty-two original hymns, half of which Beissel himself had composed. Finally, in 1730, Beissel contracted with Franklin to print a book on matrimony, extolling Hochmann's view of celibacy as the highest form of Christian life commitment.

Franklin, in his autobiography, recalled an encounter with Wohlfahrt (whom he called "Wellfare"). Franklin claimed that he met Wohlfahrt shortly after the founding of the "Dunkers" and heard his complaints that the German Baptists

> . . . were grievously calumniated by the zealots of other persuasions, and charg'd with abominable principles and practices, to which they were utter strangers. I told him this had always been the case with new sects, and that, to put a stop to such abuse, I imagin'd it might be well to publish the articles of their belief, and the rules of their discipline. He said that it had been propos'd among them, but not agreed to, for this reason: "When we were first drawn together as a society," says he, "it had pleased God to enlighten our minds so far as to see that some doctrines, which we once esteemed truths, were errors; and that others, which we had esteemed errors, were real truths. From time to time He has been pleased to afford us farther light, and our principles have been improving, and our errors diminishing. Now we are not sure that we are arrived at the end of this progression, and at the perfection of spiritual or theological knowledge; and we fear that, if we should once print our confession of faith, we should feel ourselves as if bound and confin'd by it, and perhaps be unwilling to receive farther improvement, and our successors still more so, as conceiving what we their elders and founders had done, to be something sacred, never to be departed from."
>
> This modesty in a sect is perhaps a singular instance in the history of mankind, every other sect supposing itself in possession of all truth, and that those who differ are so far in the wrong; like a man traveling in foggy weather, those at some distance before him on the road he sees wrapped up in the fog, as well as those behind him, and also the people in the fields on each side, but near him all appears clear, tho' in truth he is as much in the fog as any of them.[2]

Although the style of Wohlfahrt's comments is more like Franklin's than Wohlfahrt's, Alexander Mack could scarcely quarrel with much of what was said, for he was in substantial agreement with most of Wohlfahrt's and Beissel's beliefs.

This controversy was in no way the only concern of Mack's ministry. Most of his time was devoted to traditional pastoral pursuits: preaching, teaching, visiting the sick, and performing the rituals of the church. To his new congregation, he expressed the same compassionate concern he had shown his people in Germany and Holland. The people responded and honored him with their joy and love.

As he ministered to his congregation, Mack soon became well acquainted with Germantown, a small village of approximately three hundred persons. Founded in 1683 by Francis Daniel Pastorius and a group of German Quakers, it had become a rather cosmopolitan town of Germans, Dutch, English, French, and Scandinavian settlers. It consisted of a single street, two miles long, with its houses all facing the main highway, which was known as the "Great Road" or the "Philadelphia Road." This street was unpaved and in a hopeless condition during rainy weather. Folklore recounts the disappearance of both horses and wagons into its swampy morass during very wet weather and tells of residents saddling horses in order to cross the street for a friendly visit. In summer, the soil of the road became a fine, choking dust, and in winter a sticky, impossible sea of mud.

Many of Germantown's houses were built of logs, with clapboards used for roofs and ceilings. Some of the settlers added a thick layer of dirt on top of the ceiling for thermal insulation. Some packed the dirt smooth and level to provide floors. For windows, slots between the logs flanked by wooden shutters often sufficed. Each house had a large fireplace built of stone or wood. Around 1700, the settlers had begun to build houses with local stone found only in a limited area near Germantown.[3]

The Becker and Gumre houses were located one-half mile north of Germantown proper in a small settlement called Beggarstown. Near the Becker home, George Bensell, a prosperous Swedish merchant, was having a two and one-half-story stone duplex built, past which Mack frequently walked, watching the construction.[4] As Mack observed life in the community and became acquainted with his new neighbors, he must have felt deep gratitude daily for the cordial welcome he and his people had received. These new neighbors were genuinely glad for the arrival of the "Dunker" families, whom they sometimes called "Tunkers" or "Dunkards."

At the north end of old Germantown, and in some open fields, stood a small log meetinghouse built by the Mennonites in 1708—the first Mennonite church in the New World. In the next block stood the "Wyck" house, built in 1690; nine generations of the same family were to live beneath its roof. It was a handsome stone house, built by Caspar Wistar, who established the first glass factory in the colonies.

Several blocks farther stood the Friends meetinghouse, built of stone in 1705. This building served as a construction model for both the Mennonite and the German Baptist stone meetinghouses, both of which were built in 1770. Most of the Germantown Quakers were Dutch-speaking Germans from Krefeld and Krisheim in the lower Rhine valley.

Mack most certainly became acquainted with John Bechtel, a native of Heidelberg, who had arrived in Pennsylvania in 1726. Having received a license to preach from Heidelberg University, Bechtel held Reformed services in his home. Mack and Bechtel may have discussed the differences in their faith, but Mack did not persuade him to become a Baptist. In 1740, however, Bechtel did leave the Reformed church to join the Moravian Brethren.

Since Mack's work experience in Schriesheim had been with the milling trade, he must have found Germantown a most interesting place. Besides the Townsend gristmill, there were other mills located on the Wissahickon Creek and its tributaries. A Mennonite preacher, the first in America, had built the Rittenhouse papermill in 1690. Located on the Monoshone Creek, it provided paper for the Bradford, Franklin, and Sauer presses. At least one other papermill was located directly on the Wissahickon. One of the sawmills in the area fronted on the Wissahickon on John Gumre's property, providing lumber for expanding Germantown.

As much as Mack may have enjoyed the bustling, busy economy of this rather unique little village, his most satisfying moments came at the close of the day when he sat down to study his Bible[5] and to read from a few of the devotional books he had brought from the Old World. Reading materials in German were very scarce, being limited to costly books and journals imported from Europe. Seven different almanacs were for sale in Philadelphia when Mack arrived, but they were all in English. Both the *Pennsylvania Gazette,* published by Benjamin Franklin, and the *American Weekly Mercury,* published by Andrew Bradford, the two available newspapers, were printed in

English.

In 1731, the first German almanac appeared, *Der Teutsche Pilgrim,* published by Andreas Bradford. In 1732, Benjamin Franklin began to publish a German translation of his *Pennsylvania Gazette,* the *Philadelphische Zeitung.* It folded after the second issue.

Although few German Baptists could read English, they learned the news by word of mouth, and quickly. In the week that Mack arrived, he heard reports that all Protestants were being evicted from the Canary Islands, that the Inquisition had condemned an agéd Portuguese man to the galleys for three years, and that Governor Burnett of Boston had died.

Some news spread without the help of a newspaper. All of the Brethren in Conestoga, Coventry, and Germantown heard of one Conestoga farmer's bout with a panther, a story which made them more aware of some of the dangers they faced. This farmer saw a big panther among his swine, and rushed out with his dogs, which successfully treed it. When the farmer brought a neighbor to kill the cat with his gun, the cat was merely wounded in the front legs. It sprang from the tree, leaping upon the farmer. Once again the dogs attacked, and the neighbor was able to shoot the panther in the head.

Mack had been informed that wolves were often sighted in the area, and that a bear had been shot on the "Great Road" just a few months before.

On September 25, 1729, the *Pennsylvania Gazette* carried a news item which greatly disturbed the sensitive and compassionate Mack. Two white men, one white woman, and one mulatto woman had been sentenced to death for running away from their masters. The *American Mercury* of the same day published the following advertisement:

> To be sold: a likely Negro Man in Market Street next door to the sign of the Hat.

And in the same newspaper for April 16, 1730, appeared the following:

> There is to be sold very reasonably a very likely Negro woman, who has lived in Philadelphia from her childhood, and speaks very good English. She can do all sorts of House Work, as Washing of a house, Washing of Cloaths, Starching, Scouring Pewter, and the like; she can Knit and Sew, Spin Flax, Cotton, Worsted and Wool very well. There is to be sold with her a very likely Negroe Boy, between two and three years old.

In neither Germany nor Holland had Mack ever confronted the buying and selling of slaves. In Pennsylvania, however, it was a rather common practice. The Germantown Quakers and Mennonites, though, did not approve. A group of Quakers had already met in the home of Tunes Kunders, as early as 1688, to make the first public protest in America against the slave trade. When this protest was submitted to the English-speaking Quakers of Philadelphia, however, it met with disapproval, for many of their families owned slaves.

The indenture system was a form of slavery, for the master had complete control over a person's life until his debt was discharged. In the month that Mack arrived, William Dewees of Germantown offered a twenty-shilling reward for the capture of his runaway man-servant, Melchizedek Arnold, of "middle stature and reddish curled hair."[6]

Shortly before Mack's arrival, one of Germantown's more prominent citizens built a house at the extreme southern end of the village. In January 1730, he inserted the following advertisement in the *Pennsylvania Gazette:*

> Run away about the last day of November past from John Naglee of Germantown . . . a Dutch Servant named Johannes Fetterly, who speaks very little English . . . age about 34 years. . . . 3 pounds reward.

Mack was genuinely disturbed by the issue of slavery in the New World, but he was relieved to find very little crime in Germantown. He soon discovered, though, that such was not the case in Philadelphia. In September 1729, a James Smith received a death sentence for burglary. Several weeks later three felons were "whipped around the town" with thirty-five lashes; and the April 30, 1730, issue of the *American Weekly Mercury* printed this advertisement:

> Whereas Christ-Church in Philadelphia was broke open on Monday or Tuesday night, the 20th or 21st Instant, by some Prophane Wretches, who like Brutes abused some things belonging to said church, and stole from the Reading Desk, one large Bible, and one Common Prayer Book in Folio, and another in Octavo. This is to give notice, that whoever will discover the authors of such villany, so as he, or they, may be brought to Justice shall be amply rewarded by the Church Wardens of said Church.

Germantown was not besieged by burglary (Mack felt no need to lock his front door), but it had its share of work-related accidents: people being viciously kicked by horses, falling off ladders, or cutting themselves with knives. In the summer of 1730, one young girl caught her hand in an apple-cider mill. Although her entire arm was drawn into the machine, and ground off, she survived.[7] On another occasion, the *Pennsylvania Gazette* reported that "one, Jacob Koffman, driving his team through [Germantown] accidentally fell down, and the wheel passing over his head crushed it so that he died instantly."[8] These were the hazards of life in the colonies, and details of such accidents were amply supplied by the newspapers.

Of more interest to Mack than the accidents and the gossip of Germantown were the significant events in the life of his family and of his extended family, the church. In 1730 or 1731 he officiated at the wedding of his son, John Valentine, to Maria Hildebrand. Maria's parents, John and Maria, had come to America with Peter Becker and had been present at the first love feast in 1723. In 1732, Mack was pleased by the arrival of a new granddaughter, named Elizabeth.

This marriage did not bring all happiness into the Mack family. Some strain began to appear when Maria began to develop feelings of guilt over being married. Having spent some time with Beissel earlier, she became increasingly attracted to the mystical, celibate aspects of his teaching.

Ready to build his own house, Mack and two of his sons purchased a half-acre of land near the site of the present Germantown church. There they constructed a double log house.[9] Alexander, Sr., and Alexander, Jr., lived on one side, while John Valentine and Maria lived on the other. At times Mack opened his new home, as he had always done, for Brethren worship services.

In 1730, Mack learned of a surprising development in Christopher Sauer's family. Sauer's wife had become quite attracted by Beissel's teaching. Finally, convinced that marriage was not compatible with the Christian life, she left her husband and their nine-year-old son to be rebaptized by Beissel and to join another woman in living a continent life. She later joined the Ephrata community as Sister Marcella.

Christopher Sauer, heartbroken and burdened by the total responsibility for his son's well-being, decided to leave Conestoga and resettle in Germantown. Although Sauer considered himself a Separatist and, like Hochmann, never joined a church, he had a very high regard for the "Old Brethren" in Germantown and was understandably resentful toward Conrad Beissel of Conestoga.

In Germantown, Sauer renewed his friendship with Mack, whom he had previously known in Schwarzenau. On occasions he worshiped with the Baptists, for he had known many of them in Europe. Noticing their need for space, Sauer decided to build his own house with a second story, equipping it with moveable partitions for the use of the Baptists; they met in his house until 1758, the year in which Christopher Sauer died.

Becker, Sauer, and Mack became close companions, and felt great concern over Beissel's efforts to discredit their beliefs. A letter to Becker from Beissel stated that " . . . in those [matters] which concern your mode of divine worship, I can take no part."[10] Mack was especially pained by this letter. He had carefully studied the Bible and felt that the Baptist mode of worship was truly according to New Testament examples. He sincerely wanted it to be. In spite of Beissel's very evident attitudes of spiritual superiority, Mack felt led by God to follow the guidance of Matthew 18 and seek a reconciliation.

Mack had no interest in asserting ecclesiastical authority. He was not tempted to dominate a rival. He was, however, determined to protect the institution and save it from the forays of a charismatic revolutionary. Once again, the irony of his position must have crossed his mind, for he was now in the position of Pastor Agricola of Schriesheim, who had attempted to save his church from the influence of the young Alexander Mack.

The doctrinal differences between Beissel and Mack were trivial. On the question of the Sabbath, the Baptist Brethren, at least at first, had an open mind. Celibacy was not a weighty issue, for the Brethren respected the right of the individual to choose his own life-style, celibacy or marriage.

The basic problem between Mack and Beissel concerned community. Beissel had broken the community. He had severed the fellowship by repudiating his baptism and was developing his own distinct community at Ephrata, later to be known as the Ephrata Cloisters. Mack's continuing intention was to reconcile the Baptist movement so that the Baptists could all live together in unity of spirit once again.

Beissel felt that his was the biblical position, that he was more nearly true to the Schwarzenau *Täufer* than were the tradition-bound Germantown Baptists. When Beissel had heard that Mack was migrating to America, he may have hoped that Mack would join with him as being the more authentically Christian interpreter of the scrip-

tures. However, when Mack finally made an effort in 1730 to arrange
a meeting with him, Beissel did not appear.

In October of the same year, Mack made a pastoral visit to
Falckner's Swamp (near Pottstown), where a number of Baptists met
regularly for worship. By chance Conrad Beissel and a number of
Conestoga Brethren also traveled to the Swamp, where they were invited to a service of worship in John Senseman's house. When Mack
arrived, and learned of this meeting, he decided to attend. Hoping for
reconciliation, Mack entered the room, giving a customary greeting
among Pietists, "The peace of the Lord be with you!" The group was,
however, offended by Mack's entrance, considering it an interruption
of their worship while forgetting how they themselves had interrupted
Quaker services in Philadelphia. Beissel, although truly desiring the
blessing of this respected and "venerable patriarch," had concluded
that Mack's loyalty must certainly now lie with the Germantown Baptists since he had lived with them more than a year. Perhaps out of
fear of Mack's disapproval, Beissel had become reticent to meet with
him.

Persisting in his attempts to reconcile the Brethren to one
another, Mack inquired of the visitors from Ephrata why they had
felt called to put the Germantown Brethren under the ban. Receiving
no answer, he called the group to prayer to seek God's help in healing this festering wound in the church.

Kneeling, with walking sticks in their hands, the Germantown
Brethren led in the prayers, appealing for mutuality, friendship,
penitence, and reconciliation. The Conestoga Brethren were offended
by Mack's assumption of leadership. Unable to restrain himself,
young Michael Wohlfahrt interrupted the prayers, sarcastically cry-
ing out: "Call loudly, call loudly; perhaps your God is asleep."[11]

Mack, perhaps disconcerted, and not recognizing Beissel from
the past, asked, "Which one of you is Conrad Beissel?" The leader of
the group answered, "I am the man." Humbly and patiently, Mack
sought to inquire why the Conestoga group had so grievously severed
the fellowship.

Beissel became greatly disturbed. Although he could easily
denounce many of the Germantown Brethren, even Peter Becker, as
his spiritual inferiors, he could not so readily attack Mack. He felt indebted to Mack for much of his own religious heritage. Yet, he was
angered that Mack had placed him in an awkward defensive position
through public interrogation. Petulantly, he protested against Mack's

interruption of the meeting, after which he refused to say another word.

The impetuous Wohlfahrt was more voluble. He argued loudly and at length with the Germantown Brethren, denouncing them for not observing the Sabbath, not accepting Beissel's prophetic leadership, and failing to fulfill the Schwarzenau dream of a celibate community. These arguments became so acrimonious that one eyewitness reported that "on both sides words were uttered which are better not repeated."[12]

When the tumult subsided, both sides were chagrined that a desire for reconciliation had become an experience of increased alienation. In a moment of contrition, one of Beissel's followers called out to Mack as he was leaving, "I consider you to be a servant of God."[13]

Following his return to Germantown, Mack sadly considered the division he had seen in America. Wanting to explain his position, he wrote a tract reasoning that if the church is to survive it must maintain some kind of unity through orderly congregational governance. In Mack's view, Beissel had no authority to initiate arbitrarily the observance of the seventh day of the week as the holy day. Perhaps Mack also wanted to answer Beissel's charge that Mack had once stated: "We now lack nothing any more except the Sabbath, but we have enough to bear already."[14] Mack, furthermore, objected to Beissel's modifying the love feast by having only the minister administer the bread and the cup. The German Baptist Brethren had traditionally broken the bread for one another. If the Conestoga group were a completely separate entity, Mack would have no objection to whatever they might do. But since they claimed to be a part of the German Baptist fellowship, they should abide by the German Baptist practices. After all, each tribe has a right to maintain its own standards, Mack contended.[15]

Mack's concern over the Beissel situation was temporarily relieved when he was able to welcome Luke Vetter and three of his children to Pennsylvania on September 21, 1731. Luke Vetter was one of the original eight New Baptists. Except for George Grebe, all of the surviving participants in that first baptismal service were now in America. One of Vetter's children and his wife had died in Europe.

A ship's arrival was always a time for rejoicing. Not all the ships from Rotterdam, however, reached their destination. In February 1732, news of the tragic fate of a Rotterdam ship reached Germantown. Filled with German emigrants bound for Philadelphia, the ship had been blown off course. After twenty-four weeks at sea, it landed finally at Martha's Vineyard, a small island off the coast of New England. During the last eight weeks, food was extremely scarce. A pint of porridge was the daily allowance for five persons. Of the one hundred fifty original passengers, only fifty survived the voyage, and within three days after landing fifteen more died. Although the captain of this vessel was tried by the courts for negligence and incompetence, he was acquitted.

A happier occasion was the arrival, on October 17, 1732, aboard the *John and William,* of an unmarried minister from Schwarzenau, Abraham Dubois.[16] He had been an assistant to Mack there, and became a prominent speaker among the German Baptists in the New World. He made his home with the Great Swamp congregation from 1738 until his death in 1748 at the age of seventy.

During these early years in Germantown, the Baptist Brethren moved frequently from one location in Pennsylvania to another, seeking economic advantages or more congenial religious communities. Daniel Ritter, one of the Marienborn Brethren, who had come to Pennsylvania with Peter Becker, moved with several other families to Oley, thirty-five miles northwest of Germantown. With Becker's support, they established a new congregation there in 1732. Mack joined eagerly in helping Becker with the organizational work of the church, but he felt an even deeper commitment to the work of reconciliation between Beissel's group and the other Baptist congregations.

On one occasion, when Beissel and Mack met accidentally, Mack again broached the subject of reconciliation. Beissel and his followers offered Mack their plan: simply allow both sides to forget everything that had happened, and the peace of Christ could be restored. Mack could not accept such a flippant proposal, for it did not come to grips with the basic problem of governance. Furthermore, Mack believed that Beissel needed to show penitence for the arrogance and pride he had exhibited through his past actions. Both groups went their separate ways, realizing that the rupture was beyond repair.

In 1732, Beissel formally organized the Ephrata community, a daring venture in communal life. Emphasizing celibacy, observing the seventh day, and developing a self-sufficient economy, it survived into the twentieth century. There were now two official groups of Baptist Brethren, the First Day Baptists with Germantown as their chief congregation, and the Seventh Day Baptists at Ephrata. Except for

their differences on the Sabbath Day, methods of serving the communion, and the practice of celibacy, the two groups were in basic
agreement. In spite of their mutual antagonism, they were closer to
each other than to any other sect or denomination in colonial
America. For many years there was considerable shifting of
membership from one group to the other.

Although Beissel never lost a measure of respect for Alexander
Mack and Peter Becker, his animosity toward the "Old Brethren" increased. Walter Klein, Beissel's biographer, wrote: "Nothing sheds
less luster upon Beissel than the perfidy he showed in association with
these people."[17]

The Germantown Brethren felt quite defensive against Beissel's
attacks, even though they sometimes admired and perhaps un-
consciously envied the spiritual zeal and the emotional intensity his
movement created. Ephrata brought to mind memories of
Schwarzenau and its early spiritual fervor.

An undercurrent of religious restlessness surfaced when Stephen
Koch began to share with the Brethren in Germantown his mystical
visions. Koch had come to Pennsylvania with Becker, and had
attended the first Baptist love feast in America. Dissatisfied with the
routine of regular worship services, he said that "the revival spirit
gradually was extinguished among them, and they [had fallen] back
upon mere external forms of divine worship . . . "[18]

Koch believed that the love feast, the prayers, the Bible readings,
and the other features of Baptist life had been instituted by God,

> . . . yet they were never meant to be the end itself, as though everything
> were fulfilled if one met once every week and heard something talked
> about which, after all, no one intends to carry out, and then devoted
> the remaining days of the week to the world.[19]

Koch became so bold as to attack the emphasis of the Brethren
on baptism:

> . . . they recognize no one as a brother who has not been baptized, even
> though he should surpass them in knowledge and experience; such a
> one has to be satisfied with the title of "friend."[20]

In expressing these ideas, Koch was perhaps unaware that he was
moving toward the position held by Beissel.

Mack had to take firm action to meet the emerging crisis in the
community. He felt that he had to protect his people from Beissel's

assaults, as he had protected the Schwarzenau Baptists against the attacking Inspirationists. Mack strongly reaffirmed his faith in the original Schwarzenau position—that the essence of Christianity is found in a responsible, disciplined community of mutual love patterned after the New Testament church. It is not found in aberrant religious excesses, mystical visions, or finely spun theologies. The true faith is found by carrying the cross of Christ into the arena of daily decision-making and action.

Mack had not forgotten the religious excitement of those early days at Schwarzenau. But at Schwarzenau, in Surhuisterveen, and again in Germantown, he labored diligently to establish the kind of communal life which expressed its faith in a stable pattern of mutual love for one another and for God. Although in his own youth Mack had trenchantly attacked the institutionalism of the Reformed Church of the Palatinate and had followed Hochmann in his enthusiastic search for Separatistic freedom, Mack and his followers at Schwarzenau soon realized that God is honored in the common events of one's daily life as well as in the ecstasy of uninhibited worship and the zeal of religious rebellion. For Mack, the stability of Christian community held high priority, and such stability required a certain amount of orderly routine.

When Koch reproached the Germantown Brethren by saying,

> It is known that the Schwarzenau Brethren at first were an awakened people, among whom the spirit of virginity had its abode . . . [but] the revival spirit gradually was extinguished among them,[21]

he was forgetting that the Schwarzenau Brethren were also a people committed to openness for new truth from God, so that they might grow "in wisdom and stature and in favor with God and man," as Christ had grown. They had tried "virginity," and had discovered through their own experience that marriage and the practice of one's faith are not incompatible.

In January 1733, Koch was profoundly affected by the death of his close friend, John Henry Traut, who had also been present at the first love feast in 1723. Observing long periods of self-examination, he began to have very intense mystical visions which he shared with others. Mack took appropriate steps to retain Koch in the fellowship, keenly aware of the power of such religious experiences.

As Mack adapted to the tension of the change within the church, he also adapted to the milieu of colonial America. Gradually he moved away from the strict exclusivism of Liebe and the early Mennonites toward a more moderate Pietistic position, a recognition that authentic Christianity is present in churches other than the German Baptist. Mack had taken essentially that position in his debate with the Inspirationist, Eberhard Gruber, in 1713. But by 1715 he had moved toward a more exclusive position, which he maintained in Holland. Perhaps a need for self-preservation was a factor at that time, but the religious freedom of colonial America may have moved Mack toward his earlier more tolerant position. Mack could scarcely preserve such exclusivism, since the house in which the Brethren worshiped had been built for their use by Christopher Sauer, a remarkable Christian Pietist, who had not been baptized by trine immersion.

When Mack first arrived in Pennsylvania, he could not speak English. Yet the intellectual curiosity and "enlightened" atmosphere of Philadelphia did not escape his attention. The scientific pursuits of Benjamin Franklin exemplified the mood of the times. Mack was not insulated from this, and wrote in his Bible:

> The learned astronomers write that the sun is 166 times larger than the entire earth and that the sun is 187,000 miles in distance above the earth and that the planet Mercury is twenty-two times larger than the earth. The planet Jupiter is ninety-five times larger than the earth and is many thousands of miles in distance above the earth. Oh, what a wonderfully great and incomprehensible Creator must He be who had created and sustained such creations.

Social patterns which affected Mack's growth at this time were much more equalitarian and accepting of diversity than any Mack had experienced in either Germany or Holland. The dedication to liberty and equality prevalent in Pennsylvania expressed itself in a laissez-faire spirit among the various religious groups which had settled there. Other dimensions of life also exemplified this attitude. Benjamin Franklin reported an incident that occurred at a public auction in Chester County:

> When a man was unreasonably abusive to his wife, the women formed themselves into a court, tried the man, and found him guilty, had him ducked three times in a pond, and had half his hair and beard cut off.[22]

It is not surprising that Mack modified his strict in-group stance under the influence of such patterns. It may be further assumed that Mack's own probing of the mind of Christ led him to a more accepting and loving attitude toward non-Brethren and those who differed with him.

By the time Mack learned of John Naas's plan to migrate to America he was aware that he had relaxed some of his strict views. Although Naas had been alienated from the Brethren at Krefeld by Liebe's legalistic position on marriage within the church, Mack had urged him to migrate to America and become reconciled to the Brethren. Naas still considered himself a minister and deeply desired to become a part of the Baptist Brethren in the New World.

When Naas and his family arrived in Philadelphia on September 29, 1733, they were warmly welcomed by Mack and other brethren and sisters from Germantown. Naas wrote back to his son in Europe:

> Brethren and sisters came to meet us in small boats with delicious bread, apples, peaches, and other refreshments of the body for which we praised the great God publicly on the ship with much singing and resounding prayers.[23]

It was a moving moment when these two church leaders embraced. The mellowing Mack apologized for the pain which the Brethren in Krefeld had caused Naas, and Naas responded that he no longer felt any bitterness toward Liebe or the others. Eager for unity of spirit, Naas looked forward to resuming his ministry among the Brethren.

For a short period of time Naas and his wife stayed with friends in Germantown—perhaps with Mack himself. He was eager to share stories with other Brethren about their voyages and his own. The Naas family had migrated on the *Pennsylvania Merchant* and had experienced one of the more disastrous ocean voyages. Five babies and three adults had died during the trip, and the voyage took more than twelve weeks. Naas himself had fallen from a ladder and had been immobilized for two weeks.

By the end of 1733, Naas resettled in Amwell, New Jersey, with four other Brethren families to establish a new congregation. Mack was pleased to anoint Naas as their bishop.

After Naas departed, Mack spent the year 1734 strengthening the Germantown church and supporting Becker with the Conestoga and Oley congregations. The Brethren congregation in Germantown was growing so rapidly that elders of the Reformed congregation in Philadelphia were deploring their losses:

> the numbers of those who . . . have gone over to the Tumplers [German Baptists], Sabbatarians [Beissel], and Mennonites and others is so large that it cannot be stated without tears in one's eyes.[24]

In spite of a rapid growth in numbers, the Germantown church leaders could not ignore Ephrata. In 1734

Michael Wohlfahrt, one of the Christian philosophers of Conestoga arrived 25 September in Philadelphia where in full market he preached against the iniquity of the inhabitants of the city.[25]

Mack was not ignorant of the appeal which Beissel's group was exerting upon some of the Germantown Brethren. More and more of them were looking upon Beissel as a promising leader who could recapture for the community the glory of Schwarzenau.

Mack was no longer a revolutionary leader. He had become the shepherd of a flock and was perhaps uncomfortable in the contradiction of his original role. The insoluble problem of Beissel's defection preyed on Mack's spirit and undermined his health.[26]

On February 19, 1735, to the deep sorrow of his brothers and sisters in the faith, and also of many of Beissel's followers and Germantown Separatists, Alexander Mack died. Notices were promptly sent to all of the surrounding congregations, inviting them to attend his funeral.

The services began with a noonday meal provided by the Germantown congregation. Mack's coffin, made of choice walnut wood, was placed in the "big room" of his house, where his body could be viewed. The house could not hold everyone who attended. In spite of the cold weather, most of the people stood outside. The Pietistic hymn-singing and preaching lasted until sundown. From his knowledge of Pennsylvania-German funerals, Julius Sachse described the funeral procession:

. . . When darkness had fairly set in a cortege was formed. First came flambeau-bearers; then the carriers, four of whom bore the coffin upon their shoulders; then followed the Wissahickon brotherhood chanting the *De Profundus* alternately with the Ephrata contingent, who sang a hymn specially composed for the occasion. The rear was brought up by the relatives, friends, and Germantown Brethren.

It was an impressive and weird sight as the cortege, with its burden and flickering torches filed with slow and solemn step down the old North Wales road. A walk of about a quarter of a mile brought them to a graveyard. It was merely a small field, half an acre in extent.

The graveyard was known as the Upper Burying Ground, and was open to all, regardless of faith.

When the procession arrived at the grave, the sight was an inspiring one, worthy of the artist's brush—the hermits and the brethren in their peculiar garb, with uncovered heads and long flowing beards chanting their requiem; the snow-covered ground; the flickering torches; the coffin upon its rude bier; the black, yawning grave, and the starlit canopy above. As the mourners surrounded the grave another dirge was sung while the body was lowered into its resting place.[27]

Sometime before his death, Mack had said to his sons: "Now when I am gone, don't mark my grave, or they might sometime want to erect a monument. ... "[28] Mack's sons were distressed and protested to their father. At last Mack agreed to allow them to mark his grave with a small slab.

The Upper Burying Ground was later abandoned. In 1894, over one hundred fifty years after Mack's death, the Reverend George N. Falkenstein, pastor of the Germantown Church of the Brethren, arranged for the body to be moved to the cemetery back of the church, where six generations of Mack descendants were also buried.

After his father's death, Alexander Mack, Jr., went into a deep depression, even anticipating his own imminent death. In 1737, he joined the mystic, Stephen Koch, in establishing a monastery on the Wissahickon Creek. During the year 1738 he entered Beissel's Ephrata community, where he participated in a symbolic rebaptism for his dead father.

That same year, John Valentine Mack and his wife and daughter, with about fifteen others from Germantown, also joined the Ephrata Brethren.

The religious appeal of Ephrata for Mack's sons is not surprising. Perhaps they were seeking to recover the spiritual zeal of the New Baptists in Europe as they remembered it. Perhaps they had been drawn in this direction for some time, but, honoring their father, had remained loyal to the Germantown congregation during his lifetime. Whatever their motivation, they were searching, as Mack himself had searched, for a meaningful faith.

John Valentine never left the Ephrata community, but Alexander Mack, Jr., soon came to his father's realization that God can just as well be honored through one's daily life as in mystic contemplation. In 1745 he left Ephrata and returned to Germantown, where for many years he served as the bishop of the New Baptist congregation.

Although this "venerable patriarch" of the church had died at the comparatively early age of fifty-six, his influence on the people

The original marker, Alexander Mack's grave.

touched by his life is an eloquent testimony to the kind of life he lived, to the magnificence of his vision of life in community unspoiled by violence, and to the sincerity of his conviction that God's Spirit is best manifested in practical, concrete, human relationships of Christian love.

Alexander Mack was a truly humble man, and out of his humility he fashioned the most precious gift he could leave his spiritual progeny: a vision of life always open to new guidance by God through Christ, to new understandings of truth, and to new expressions of faith.

If, in his illness, he uttered prayers for his brethren and sisters, he certainly would have prayed that they love one another, keeping ever before them the vision of a community ruled by God in love and peace, rather than by man in greed and violence.

> All those on whose hearts the law of God is written are united in the one faith, the one baptism, and the one spirit in accordance with Jesus Christ. This is the perfect will of the true law-giver that they who are His should be one even as the Father and the Son are one.[29]

And, if in his last days his memories turned back to his wife and two daughters buried in Europe, to the loss of his homeland, and to the alienation from his family in Schriesheim, Mack may have counseled the friends who gathered around his bed:

> If you have learned from Him the teaching as it is outwardly commanded in the [New] Testament, so that you will remain steadfast in it, and resolve yourself to sacrifice your life, your property, family, yes, all that you have in the whole world . . . you must become used to taking his cross upon yourself daily. . . . [30]

Mack must have pondered deeply the drastic changes which had occurred in his own lifetime. As a young man he had made a "covenant of good conscience". with God. During his lifetime he had "counted the cost" many times, had "fought a good fight," and had remained faithful to the transcendent vision he had received of the human possibilities within a disciplined, supportive, Christ-centered community. Confident also in the mysterious realm existing beyond human life, he could proclaim:

> Blessings and glories of such great dignity will be obtained through Christ that no human tongue can express it, nor can be described what God has prepared for those who love him.[31]

APPENDIX

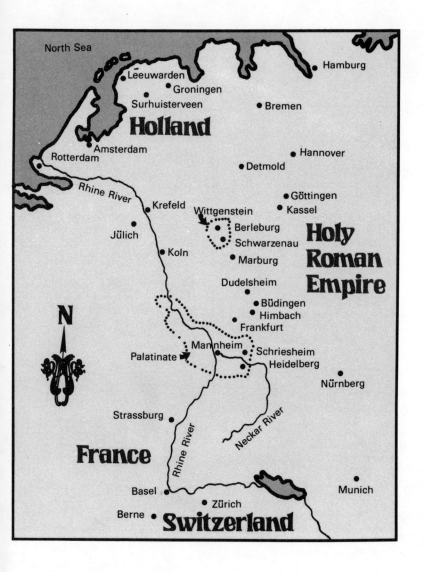

Map of 18th Century Germany

CHRONOLOGY
764-1735
AM-Alexander Mack

764 c.	Schriesheim founded.
1560 c.	Ebert Mack settles in Schriesheim, purchases mill. (AM's great-great-grandfather)
1574 c.	Hieronymus Mack born. (AM's great-grandfather)
1594	Ebert Mack appointed mayor of Schriesheim.
1610	George Mack born. (AM's grandfather)
1612 c.	Ebert Mack dies.
1618-1648	Thirty Years War.
1624-1625	Hieronymus Mack serves as local judge.
1625	Typhus epidemic in Schriesheim.
1630 c.	Hieronymus Mack dies.
1632	Mill destroyed. Mack family loses possession.
1636	John Philip Mack born. (AM's father)
1648	Treaty of Westphalia.
1655-1685	George Mack serves as mayor of Schriesheim.
1672	John Philip marries Christina Fillbrun. He purchases house next to Schwengel fountain.
1672-1679	"Dutch War"
1674	Large portion of Schriesheim burned.
1675	Agricola appointed Reformed pastor of Schriesheim.
1679	June 27. John Philip Mack re-purchases "Mack Mill."
1679	AM born. July 27 baptized in local church.
1683	Germantown founded by Pastorius.
1686-1697	War of the Grand Alliance.
1689	John Philip Mack, AM's oldest brother, dies.

1690-1691 John Philip Mack, AM's father, serves as mayor.

1690 c. Anna Margaret Mack, AM's sister, married to John Caspar Bayer.

1692 AM confirmed in local church.

1693 Heidelberg destroyed by fire.

1701 January 18. AM married to Anna Margaret Kling.

1701 November 13. AM's first son christened.

1702 AM's mother dies.

1702 John Jacob, AM's older brother, is married.

1702 John Philip, AM's father, wills his property to his children.

1702-1716 War of the Spanish Succession.

1703 April 19. AM's second son christened: John.

1703-1705 AM participates in Pietistic gatherings.

1705 c. AM becomes a follower of Hochmann.

1706 March 5. AM sells his half of mill to his brother.

1706 June 2. John Philip Mack, AM's father, dies.

1706 Early August. Hochmann arrives in Schriesheim for preaching mission.

1706 August 22. Pietistic meeting in Mack mill is broken up by the authorities. AM and family flee Schriesheim.

1706 September 8. AM visits Hochmann in Mannheim jail.

1706 September 14. Palatinate government outlaws Pietism.

1706 December (?). AM and family settle in Schwarzenau.

1707 AM travels on preaching missions with Hochmann.

1707 October 12. Hochmann imprisoned in Nürnberg jail.

1708 May 1. John Valentine Kling, AM's father-in-law, arrested for Pietistic activity.

1708 Early Summer (?). Two "foreign brethren" visited Schwarzenau to advocate adult, immersionist baptism.

1708 July 4. AM sends letter on subject of baptism to Hochmann.

1708 July 24. Hochmann answers AM letter, giving qualified approval to baptism.

1708 Between August 5 and 8. Public baptism of eight people in Eder River. Organization of Schwarzenau congregation.

1708 September (?). First New Baptist love feast.

1708 October. Hochmann released from Nürnberg prison.

1709 January. AM makes complete break with Hochmann.

1709 Mack travels on preaching missions.

1710	February 5. Count Charles Louis produces "Enclosure Q" attacking the New Baptists.
1711	August 21. AM's first baptism at Düdelsheim.
1711	September 5. AM's letter to Count Charles August defending the widow Hoffman.
1711	October 13. AM's second baptismal service at Düdelsheim.
1712	January 25. Birth of Alexander Mack, Jr., in Schwarzenau.
1712	November 4. AM's third baptismal service in Düdelsheim.
1713	July. Publication of AM's first tract: *Basic Questions*.
1714	June 6. Christian Liebe sentenced to galleys.
1714	John Valentine Kling, AM's father-in-law, dies.
1714	November 6. Founding of Community of True Inspiration at Himbach.
1714	Christina Mack, AM's fourth child, is born in Schwarzenau.
1715	Summer. New Baptists driven out of Marienborn area.
1715	Mack publishes second tract: *Rights and Ordinances*.
1715	The Community of True Inspiration established in Schwarzenau.
1716	April 8. Christian Liebe released from galleys.
1717	February 1. Solingen Brethren imprisoned.
1717	Fall. Häcker controversy in Krefeld.
1719	July. Peter Becker's group departs for America.
1719	Spring (?). AM visits the six Solingen Brethren in Jülich fortress.
1719	"Needy Schwarzenauers" receive 8,000 guilders from Dutch Collegiants.
1720	*Geistreiches Gesangbuch* published by Berleburg Press for the New Baptists.
1720	Early Spring. Count August David complains about the New Baptists and other dissenters.
1720	April (?). AM sells his house to Christopher Sauer.
1720	May (?). The New Baptists leave Schwarzenau for Holland.
1720	June (?). The New Baptists arrive at Surhuisterveen in Friesland.
1720	September. Anna Margaret Mack, AM's wife, and Christina, his daughter, die within a week of each other.
1720	October. Solingen Brethren released.

1721	January 12. Hochmann dies in Schwarzenau.
1721	April 28. AM marries John Juriens and Anna Kipping.
1723	December. Germantown church organized. First baptism and love feast in America.
1724	AM performs two weddings.
1724	Beissel baptized. Coventry and Conestoga churches organized.
1725	AM performs three weddings, including that of his son John to Joanna Margaret Suderein.
1727	AM's three sons travel to Schriesheim to settle estate of John Valentine Kling.
1728	Alexander Mack, Jr., baptized.
1729	May or June (?). AM with about thirty families leaves Surhuisterveen for Rotterdam.
1729	Late June. New Baptists board *Allen* at Rotterdam.
1729	July 7. *Allen* sets sail from Cowes on Isle of Wight.
1729	September 15. Arrival of *Allen* in Philadelphia.
1730	John Mack purchases one-half acre of land in Germantown.
1730	AM accepted as bishop at Germantown.
1730	AM confronts Beissel at Falckner's Swamp.
1731 c.	John Valentine Mack marries Maria Hildebrand.
1731	Luke Vetter and three children arrive in Philadelphia.
1732	Elizabeth born to John Valentine and Maria Mack.
1732	October 17. Abraham Dubois arrives in Philadelphia.
1732	Oley church organized.
1733	John Naas with family arrives in Philadelphia.
1734 c.	Final rupture between Beissel and Mack.
1734	Amwell, N. J., church organized.
1734	Fall (?). AM's health begins to fail.
1735	February 19. AM dies.
1735	February 21 (?). Funeral service for AM.
1894	AM's body transferred to its present location.

GENEALOGY

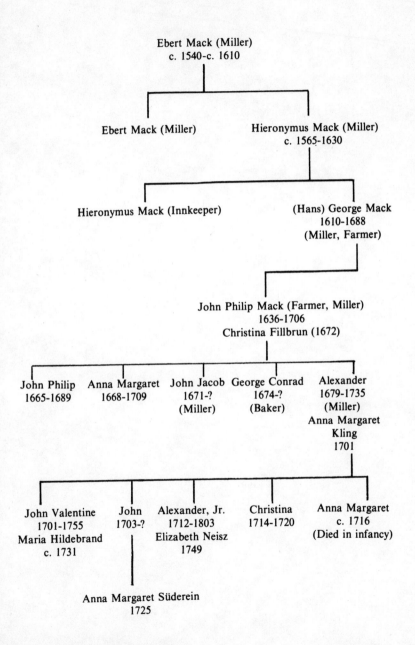

Ebert Mack (Miller)
c. 1540-c. 1610

Ebert Mack (Miller)

Hieronymus Mack (Miller)
c. 1565-1630

Hieronymus Mack (Innkeeper)

(Hans) George Mack
1610-1688
(Miller, Farmer)

John Philip Mack (Farmer, Miller)
1636-1706
Christina Fillbrun (1672)

John Philip
1665-1689

Anna Margaret
1668-1709

John Jacob
1671-?
(Miller)

George Conrad
1674-?
(Baker)

Alexander
1679-1735
(Miller)
Anna Margaret
Kling
1701

John Valentine
1701-1755
Maria Hildebrand
c. 1731

John
1703-?

Alexander, Jr.
1712-1803
Elizabeth Neisz
1749

Christina
1714-1720

Anna Margaret
c. 1716
(Died in infancy)

Anna Margaret Süderein
1725

WORKS IN REFERENCE

American Weekly Mercury.
Newspaper published in Philadelphia by Andrew Bradford.

Brumbaugh, Martin Grove.
A History of the German Baptist Brethren in Europe and America. Mount Morris, Illinois: Brethren Publishing House, 1899.

Brunn, Hermann.
1200 Jahre Schriesheim. Mannheim, Germany: Südwestdeutsche Verlagsanstalt, 1964.
400 Jahre Evangelische Gemeinde Schriesheim: 1556-1956. Weinheim/Bergstrasse: Gebrücler Diesbach, 1956.

Schriesheimer Mühlen in Vergangenheit und Gegenwart: Ein Beitrage zur Ortgeschichte. Manheim: Wilh. Burger, 1947.

Commonwealth of Pennsylvania, *Pennsylvania Archives,* Vol. XVII. (Second Series).

Durnbaugh, Donald.
Brethren Beginnings: The Origins of the Church of the Brethren in Early Eighteenth-Century Europe. Philadelphia: Unpublished dissertation for University of Pennsylvania, 1960.

The Brethren in Colonial America. Elgin, Illinois: The Brethren Press, 1967.

European Origins of the Brethren. Elgin, Illinois: The Brethren Press, 1958.

Falkenstein, George Ness.
History of the German Baptist Brethren Church. Lancaster, Pennsylvania: The New Era Printing Company, 1901.

Franklin, Benjamin.
Autobiography of Benjamin Franklin. New York: P.F. Collier & Son, 1909.

Friedmann, Robert.
Mennonite Piety Through the Centuries: Its Genius and Its Literature. Goshen, Indiana: Mennonite Historical Society, 1949.

Goebel, Max.
Geschichte des christlichen Lebens in der rheinisch-westphälischen evangelischen Kirche. Coblenz: Karl Bädecker, 1849-1860.

Hark, J. Max (Tr).
Chronicon Ephratense: A History of the Community of Seventh Day Baptists at Ephrata, Lancaster County, Penn'a. Lancaster, Pennsylvania: S.H. Zahm & Co., 1899.

Klein, Walter C.
Johann Conrad Beissel: Mystic and Martinet (1690-1768). Philadelphia: University of Pennsylvania Press, 1942.

Kurtz, Daniel Webster.
Nineteen Centuries of the Christian Church. Elgin, Illinois: Brethren Publishing House, 1914.

Mack, Alexander.
A Short and Plain View of the Outward Yet Sacred Rites and Ordinances of the House of God. (Translated by Henry Kurtz.) Ashland, Ohio: National Sunday School Association of the Brethren Church, 1939.

Pennsylvania Gazette.
Weekly newspaper published by Benjamin Franklin in Philadelphia.

Renkewitz, Heinz.
Hochmann von Hochenau (1670-1721): *Quellenstudien zur Geschichte des Pietismus. Berichte des theologischen Seminars der Brüdergemeine in Herrnhut,* No. XII, 1934. Breslau: Marschke und Berendt, 1935.

Sachse, Julius Friedrich.
The German Sectarians of Pennsylvania (1708-1742). Philadelphia, Pennsylvania: Julius F. Sachse, 1899.

Stoeffler, Ernest F.
Continental Pietism and Early American Christianity. Grand Rapids, Michigan: Wm. B. Eerdmans Publishing Co., 1976.

NOTES

CHAPTER I

1. For most of the information in this chapter and in Chapter II, I am deeply indebted to Dr. Hermann Brunn's book: *1200 Jahre Schriesheim.*
2. Hieronymus Mack died approximately twenty years before Alexander Mack was born.
3. It was Dr. Brunn's understanding that Alexander Mack was born in this house, which today is still standing but has been remodelled into a store.

CHAPTER III

1. Hermann Brunn, *Schriesheimer Mühlen in Vergangenheit und Gegenwart: Ein Beitrag zur Ortgeschichte,* p. 112.
2. Hermann Brunn, *400 Jahre Evangelische Gemeinde Schriesheim: 1556-1956,* p. 17.
3. Donald Durnbaugh, *European Origins of the Brethren,* p. 37.
4. Alexander Mack, *A Short and Plain View of the Outward Yet Sacred Rites and Ordinances of the House of God,* p. 13. Mack's reference is in accordance with Ephesians 5:14.
5. Heinz Renkewitz, *Hochman von Hochenau (1670-1721): Quellenstudien zur Geschichte des Pietismus,* p. 1.
6. Renkewitz, *Hochman von Hochenau,* p. 20.
7. Martin Grove Brumbaugh, *A History of the German Baptist Brethren in Europe and America,* p. 22.

CHAPTER IV

1. Durnbaugh, *European Origins,* p. 52.
2. Durnbaugh, *European Origins,* p. 40.
3. Durnbaugh, *European Origins,* p. 40.
4. Durnbaugh, *European Origins,* p. 45.
5. Durnbaugh, *European Origins,* p. 46.
6. Durnbaugh, *European Origins,* p. 49.

CHAPTER V

1. Renkewitz, *Hochman von Hochenau,* p. 240.
2. Durnbaugh, *European Origins,* p. 89.
3. Durnbaugh, *European Origins,* p. 95.
4. Durnbaugh, *European Origins,* p. 103.
5. Durnbaugh, *European Origins,* p. 105.
6. They were actually "Swiss Brethren," Anabaptists who later migrated to Pennsylvania.
7. Alexander Mack, *Rites and Ordinances,* p. 15.
8. Robert Friedman, *Mennonite Piety Through the Centuries: Its Genius and Its Literature,* p. 65.
9. Matthew 28:19 ff.
10. Durnbaugh, *European Origins,* p. 116.
11. Renkewitz, *Hochman von Hochenau,* p. 243.

CHAPTER VI

1. Durnbaugh, *European Origins,* p. 113.
2. Durnbaugh, *European Origins,* p. 115.
3. Durnbaugh, *European Origins,* p. 115-120.
4. Since Hochmann wrote his letter of approval on July 24, it would have taken at least a week to reach Schwarzenau, and several days for the baptists to distribute their letter of invitation; therefore the service could hardly have been held before August 5. On August 11 the news of the baptism reached Heidelberg; therefore it could hardly have taken place after August 8.

5. Durnbaugh, *European Origins*, p. 121.
6. This was a somewhat illogical procedure as the one who did the baptizing had not himself been immersed.
7. Durnbaugh, *European Origins*, p. 408, Where the entire thirteen stanzas as translated by Ora B. Garber, may be found.

CHAPTER VII

1. Gichtel died in 1710.
2. Durnbaugh, *European Origins*, p. 129.
3. Durnbaugh, *European Origins*, p. 125.
4. Durnbaugh, *European Origins*, p. 126.
5. Durnbaugh, *European Origins*, p. 128.
6. Durnbaugh, *European Origins*, p. 129.
7. *Geistreiches Gesangbuch*.
8. Durnbaugh, *European Origins*, p. 364.
9. Durnbaugh, *European Origins*, p. 363.
10. Durnbaugh, *European Origins*, p. 338-339.
11. Durnbaugh, *European Origins*, p. 343. His attitude toward infant baptism was somewhat like George Fox's toward church steeples.
12. Durnbaugh, *European Origins*, p. 363.
13. Durnbaugh, *European Origins*, p. 363.
14. Durnbaugh, *European Origins*, p. 414.
15. Durnbaugh, *European Origins*, p. 415.
16. Durnbaugh, *European Origins*, p. 415.
17. Durnbaugh, *European Origins*, p. 376.
18. Matthew 5:34-37 KJV.
19. Durnbaugh, *European Origins*, p. 341.
20. Durnbaugh, *European Origins*, p. 131.
21. Renkewitz, *Hochman von Hochenau*, p. 410.
22. Renkewitz, *Hochman von Hochenau*, p. 410.
23. Durnbaugh, *European Origins*, p. 390.
24. Durnbaugh, *European Origins*, p. 390.
25. Durnbaugh, *European Origins*, p. 392.
26. Acts 4:32-35.
27. Renkewitz, *Hochman von Hochenau*, p. 188.
28. Durnbaugh, *European Origins*, p. 142.
29. Durnbaugh, *European Origins*, p. 141.
30. Brumbaugh, *A History of the German Baptist Brethren*, p. 177.

31. Durnbaugh, *European Origins,* p. 341.
32. Daniel Webster Kurtz, *Nineteen Centuries of the Christian Church,* p. 162.
33. Durnbaugh, *European Origins,* p. 145.
34. Durnbaugh, *European Origins,* p. 399.
35. Durnbaugh, *European Origins,* p. 347.
36. Durnbaugh, *European Origins,* p. 347.

CHAPTER VIII

1. Donald Durnbaugh, *Brethren Beginnings: The Origins of the Church of the Brethren in Early Eighteenth-Century Europe,* p. 61.
2. Durnbaugh, *Brethren Beginnings,* p. 65.
3. Durnbaugh, *European Origins,* pp. 313-314.
4. Durnbaugh, *Brethren Beginnings,* p. 65. Renkewitz, Hochmann's biographer, believed that Hochmann at one time considered adult baptism for his followers, but never instituted it. Renkewitz was, however, quite sure that Hochmann was never baptized by the Baptists, nor ever became one of them.
5. Durnbaugh, *Brethren Beginnings,* p. 65.
6. Durnbaugh, *European Origins,* p. 74.
7. Durnbaugh, *European Origins,* p. 76.
8. Durnbaugh, *European Origins,* p. 73.
9. Durnbaugh, *European Origins,* p. 75. As a matter of principle, however, they did not meet on Sunday mornings.
10. Durnbaugh, *European Origins,* p. 132.
11. Durnbaugh, *European Origins,* p. 134.
12. Durnbaugh, *European Origins,* p. 141-142. The wives of the New Baptists participated in the congregation as equals; Count Charles Louis considered this practice disrespectful to their husbands.
13. Durnbaugh, *European Origins,* p. 145.
14. Durnbaugh, *European Origins,* p. 67.
15. Durnbaugh, *European Origins,* p. 147.
16. Durnbaugh, *European Origins,* p. 142.
17. Durnbaugh, *European Origins,* p. 160.
18. This hymn was composed by Wilhelm II, Duke of Saxe-Weimar. The melody was the *Cantionale Germanicum,* Dresden, 1628, later arranged by J. S. Bach. (Author's translation).

19. Durnbaugh, *European Origins,* p. 161.
20. Durnbaugh, *European Origins,* p. 164-167.
21. Durnbaugh, *European Origins,* p. 168.
22. Either they recovered their children from Heidelberg, which is rather unlikely, or they had more children.
23. Durnbaugh, *European Origins,* p. 175.
24. Durnbaugh, *European Origins,* p. 176.

CHAPTER IX

1. Its German title is *Grundforschende Fragen.*
2. Durnbaugh, *European Origins,* p. 327.
3. Durnbaugh, *European Origins,* p. 330.
4. Durnbaugh, *European Origins,* p. 331.
5. Durnbaugh, *European Origins,* p. 333.
6. Durnbaugh, *European Origins,* p. 333.
7. Durnbaugh, *European Origins,* p. 336.
8. Durnbaugh, *European Origins,* p. 328-329.
9. Durnbaugh, *European Origins,* p. 341.
10. Durnbaugh, *European Origins,* p. 341.
11. Durnbaugh, *European Origins,* p. 342.
12. Brumbaugh, *A History of the German Baptist Brethren,* p. 131.
13. Durnbaugh, *European Origins,* p. 180.
14. Durnbaugh, *European Origins,* p. 365.
15. Durnbaugh, *European Origins,* p. 399.
16. Durnbaugh, *European Origins,* p. 399.
17. Durnbaugh, *European Origins,* p. 403.

CHAPTER X

1. Durnbaugh, *Brethren Beginnings,* p. 100.
2. Durnbaugh, *Brethren Beginnings,* p. 100.
3. Durnbaugh, *European Origins,* p. 147.
4. Durnbaugh, *Brethren Beginnings,* p. 151. Three copies are known to exist—two in Germany and one in the U.S.
5. Durnbaugh, *Brethren Beginnings,* p. 150.
6. Count Henry died in 1723, and was succeeded by Count August David.

7. In 1725 his widow and four sons migrated to Pennsylvania.

CHAPTER XI

1. Durnbaugh, *Brethren Beginnings,* p. 150.
2. By 1748, however, they had died out as a distinct group.
3. In 1850 the baptistry was removed from the church.
4. Durnbaugh, *European Origins,* p. 296. There is a tradition that Anna Margaret died in Germany. The record in Alexander Mack's Bible indicates that she died in September 1720; whereas the Brethren left Schwarzenau before June 24, 1720.
5. Mack, *A Short and Plain View,* p. 9.
6. Durnbaugh, *European Origins,* p. 295.
7. See also Hark, J. Max, *Chronicon Ephratense,* p. 25.
8. Donald Durnbaugh, *The Brethren in Colonial America,* p. 537.
9. Durnbaugh, *The Brethren in Colonial America,* p. 66.
10. Durnbaugh, *The Brethren in Colonial America,* p. 36.
11. Durnbaugh, *Brethren Beginnings,* p. 157
12. Durnbaugh, *The Brethren in Colonial America,* p. 30.
13. Durnbaugh, *The Brethren in Colonial America,* p. 35.
14. Durnbaugh, *The Brethren in Colonial America,* p. 35.
15. Durnbaugh, *The Brethren in Colonial America,* p. 39.
16. Brumbaugh, *A History of the German Baptist Brethren,* p. 93.
17. *Pennsylvania Archives,* Vol. XVII.

CHAPTER XII

1. Julius Friedrich Sachse, *The German Sectarians of Pennsylvania (1708-1742),* p. 143.
2. Benjamin Franklin, *Autobiography of Benjamin Franklin,* pp. 115-116.
3. By 1750 most of the houses were stone; whereas in Philadelphia most were built of brick.
4. This and other houses mentioned in this chapter are still standing.
5. His Bible is in the Alexander Mack Memorial Library, Bridgewater College, Virginia.
6. *Pennsylvania Gazette,* September 25, 1729.

7. *Pennsylvania Gazette,* September 3, 1730.
8. *Pennsylvania Gazette,* October 24, 1732.
9. This house was probably built during the summer of 1730.
10. Durnbaugh, *The Brethren in Colonial America,* p. 89.
11. Durnbaugh, *The Brethren in Colonial America,* p. 88.
12. Durnbaugh, *The Brethren in Colonial America,* p. 88.
13. Durnbaugh, *The Brethren in Colonial America,* p. 88.
14. Durnbaugh, *European Origins,* p. 124.
15. Unfortunately, no copy of this tract has survived.
16. The *Ephrata Chronicle* includes Dubois among those arriving in 1725.
17. Walter C. Klein, *Johann Conrad Beissel: Mystic and Martinet (1690-1768),* p. 190.
18. Durnbaugh, *The Brethren in Colonial America,* p. 91.
19. Durnbaugh, *The Brethren in Colonial America,* p. 91.
20. Durnbaugh, *The Brethren in Colonial America,* p. 91.
21. Durnbaugh, *The Brethren in Colonial America,* p. 91.
22. *Pennsylvania Gazette,* April 17, 1735.
23. Durnbaugh, *European Origins,* p. 308.
24. Ernest F. Stoeffler, *Continental Pietism and Early American Christianity,* p. 237.
25. *Pennsylvania Gazette,* September 25, 1734.
26. Brumbaugh, *A History of the German Baptist Brethren,* p. 99. Brumbaugh was convinced that the controversy with Beissel hastened Mack's death.
27. Sachse, *The German Sectarians,* pp. 219-222.
28. George Ness Falkenstein, *History of the German Baptist Brethren Church,* p. 68.
29. Durnbaugh, *European Origins,* p. 387.
30. Durnbaugh, *European Origins,* p. 404.
31. Durnbaugh, *European Origins,* p. 396.

INDEX OF PERSONS

Irace, Kathleen, 10

Joel, Peter Bucher, follower of Conrad Beissel, 125
Juriens, John, Dutch convert, 108

Kachuck, Rhoda, 10
Kalcklöser, John Henry, traveled on *Allen*, 111
Kasebier, John, Schwarzenau emigrant to Philadelphia, 115
Keymen, Susan, bride of Jacob Bossert, 111
Kipping, Anna Catherine, bride of John Juriens, 108
Kipping, Joanna, one of original eight, 58
Kipping, John, one of original eight, 58
Klein, Walter, Beissel's biographer, 136
Kling, Anna Margaret, wife of Alexander Mack, 27f
Kling, John Valentine, father-in-law of Alexander Mack, 27, 38, 50f, 92, 114
Knepper, William, one of Solingen Brethren, 110
Knepper, Veronica, bride of William Knepper, 110
Koch, Stephen, Germantown mystic, 136f, 141
Koffman, Jacob, Germantown farmer, 131
Koker, De, family, Dutch Collegiants, 117
König, Samuel, Pietistic leader in Wittgenstein, 87
Kunders, Tunes, Germantown Quaker, 130

Layen, Anna Flys, Dutch convert, 111
Lemser, Matthew, occupant of Hochmann's house, 92
Liebe, Christian, early Brethren minister, 52, 62, 92ff, 100f, 110, 137, 139
Liselotte, Princess, sister-in-law of Louis XIV, 22
Lobach, John, one of Solingen Baptists, 100
Louis XIV, king of France, 22
Lucas, Martin, refugee from Heidelberg, 39, 40, 50ff, 61, 79ff, 83, 85f
Luther, Martin, Reformation leader, 11, 64f

Mack, Alexander, "founder" of the Brethren group of churches
birth of, 18
confirmation, 19
and Heidelberg Neckar College, 21
in village school, 22
burning of Schriesheim and flight to the hills, 24
marriage to Anna Margaret Kling, 27
and Mennonites, 32
sells share in mill, 37
mission to Marienborn area, 38
flees Schriesheim, 39
migrates to Schwarzenau, 42
visits Pietistic group, 44ff
sells inheritance, 49
letter to Hochmann concerning baptism, 56
Schwarzenau baptismal service, 58
views on salvation, 65f
universal restoration, 76
controversy with Hochmann, 79
baptism at Düdelsheim, 84
letter to Count Charles, 85

INDEX OF SUBJECTS AND PLACES